CHILDREN'S ENCYCLOPEDIA

THE WORLD OF KNOWLEDGE

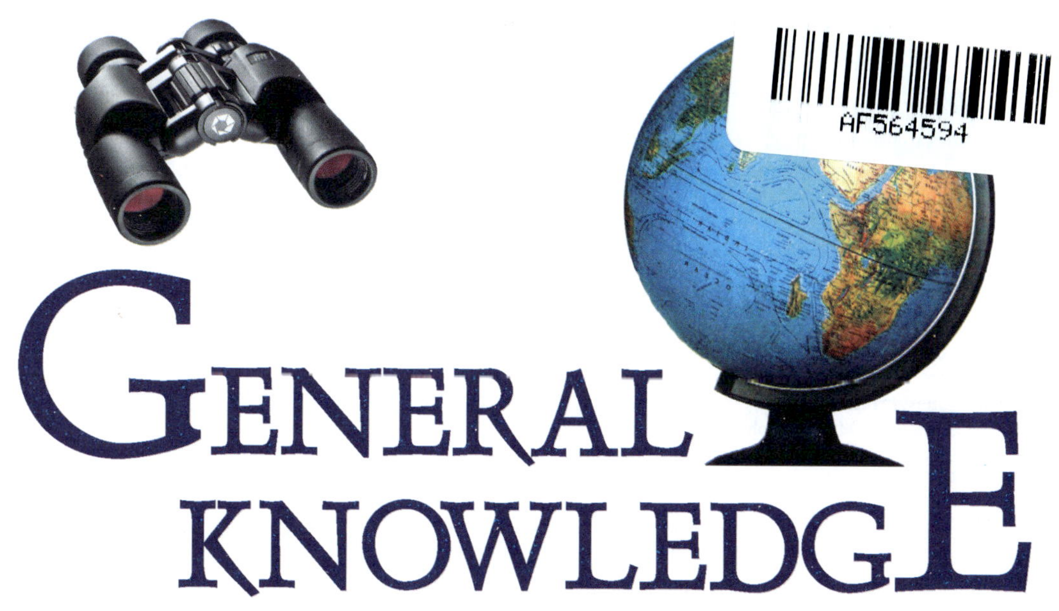

by

Manasvi Vohra

Published by:

Head Office
F-2/16, Ansari Road, Daryaganj,
New Delhi-110002 ☎ 23240026, 27, 28
info@vspublishers.com
www.vspublishers.com

Regional Office
5-1-707/1, Brij Bhawan (Beside Central
Bank of India Lane) Bank Street, Koti,
Hyderabad - 500 095 ☎ 040-24737290
vspublishershyd@gmail.com

Online Brandstore: amazon.in/vspublishers

Buy Books Online: amazon • Flipkart | **Follow us on:**    

ISBN 978-93-505704-0-1
New Edition

Cataloging in Publication Data--DK
Courtesy: D.K. Agencies (P) Ltd. <docinfo@dkagencies.com>

Vohra, Manasvi, author.
General knowledge / Manasvi Vohra. -- New edition.
pages cm. -- (Children's encyclopedia : the world of knowledge)
ISBN 9789350570401

1. Children's encyclopedias and dictionaries. I. Title. II. Series: Children's encyclopedia : the world of knowledge.

LCC AG5.V64 2024 | DDC 032 23

Printed at : Param Offsetters, Okhla, New Delhi–110020

PUBLISHER'S NOTE

V&S Publishers — Leading Publisher of Children and Academic Books in India for over a decade, is glad to announce the launch of a unique, fully *coloured set of five books* under the head, ***Children's Encyclopedia – The World of Knowledge.*** The set of 5 books namely – ***Life Sciences and the Human Body, Physics and Chemistry, Space Science and Electronics, Scientists and Inventions*** and ***General Knowledge*** has been especially developed keeping in mind the students and children of all age groups, particularly from 6 to 14 years of age. Our main aim is to arouse interest and solve queries of the school children regarding various and diverse topics of Science and help them master the subject thoroughly. After the resounding success of 71 Science Trailblazing Series, we present you with this new arrival of ours.

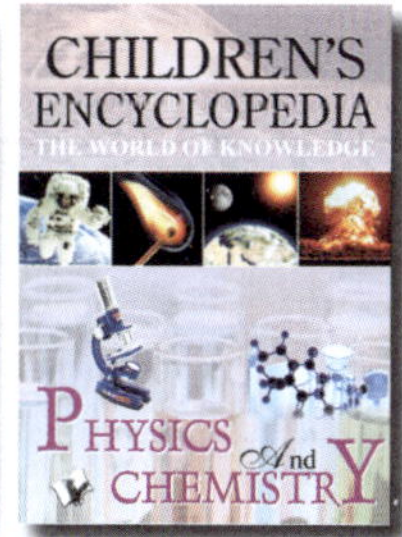

In the book, ***General Knowledge***, the author has broadly dealt with some interesting and fascinating Scientific facts in the first part (Part-I) like *The Atmosphere and its Composition, The Change of Seasons, Why do Plants and Animals become Extinct, The Vision of Owls, What is Milk made up of*, etc. The second part (Part-II), on the other hand, focusses mainly on the amazing and interesting facts of the 'World', such as: *The Stone Age, The Story behind the Name, America, How was the United Kingdom formed, What is Red Cross, The Story behind Mona Lisa* and so on...

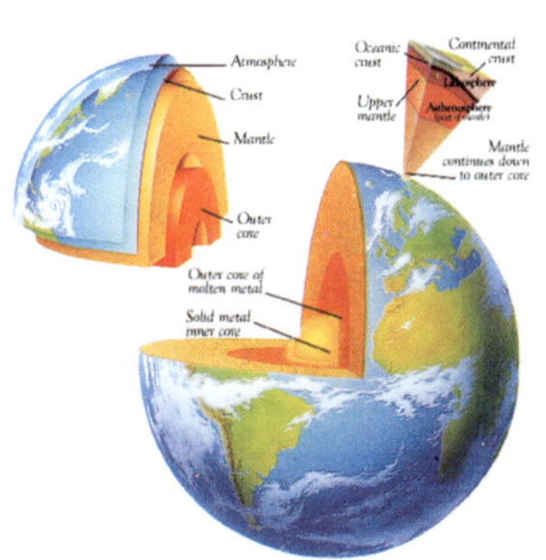

Each chapter is followed by a section called **Quick Facts** that contains a set of interesting and fascinating facts about the topics already discussed in the chapter. There are also **Exercises** compiled at the end of the book followed by a **Glossary** of difficult words and scientific terms to make the book complete and comprehensive.

Though our aim is to be flawless, but errors might have crept in inadvertently. So we request our esteemed readers to read the book thoroughly and offer valuable suggestions wherever necessary to improve and enhance the quality of the book. Hope it interests you all and serves its purpose well.

CONTENTS

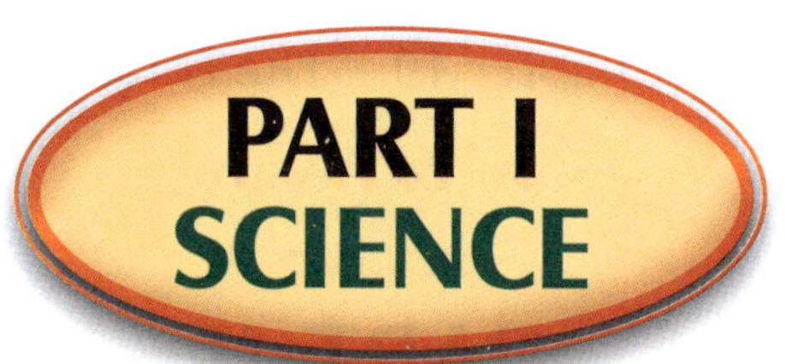

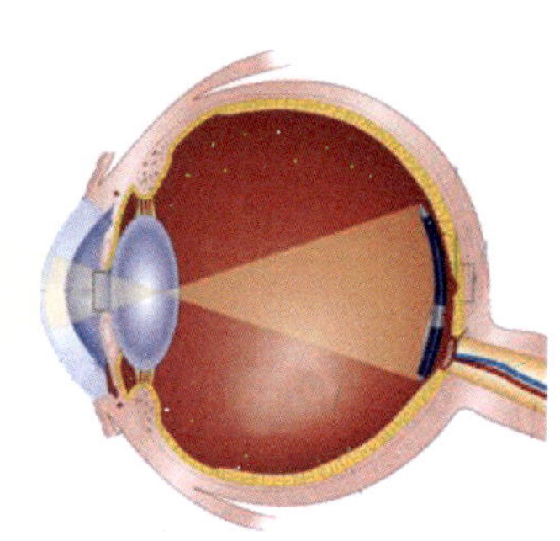

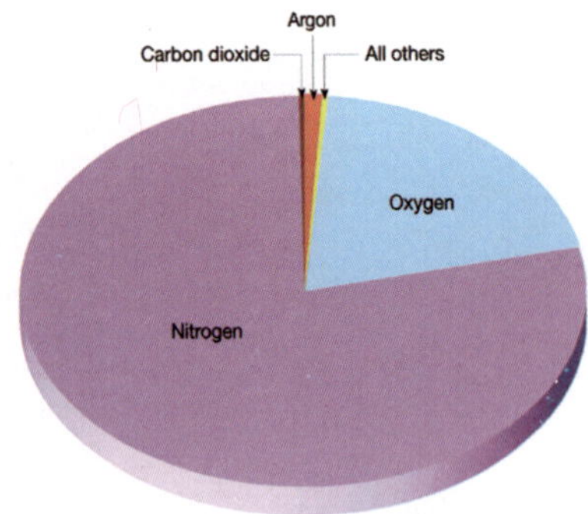

PART II THE WORLD

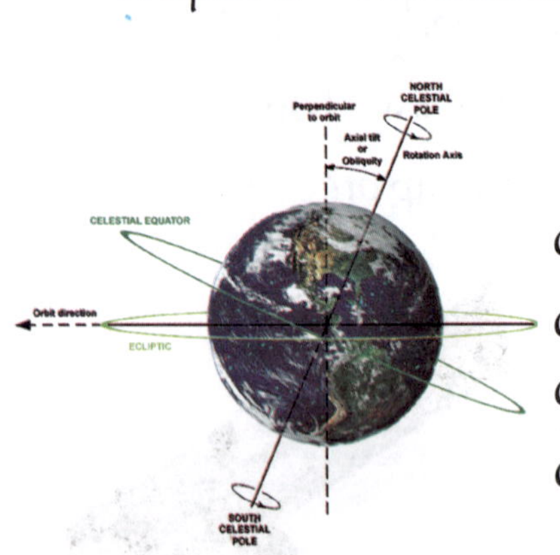

PART - I

SCIENCE

Chapter - 1

THE ATMOSPHERE

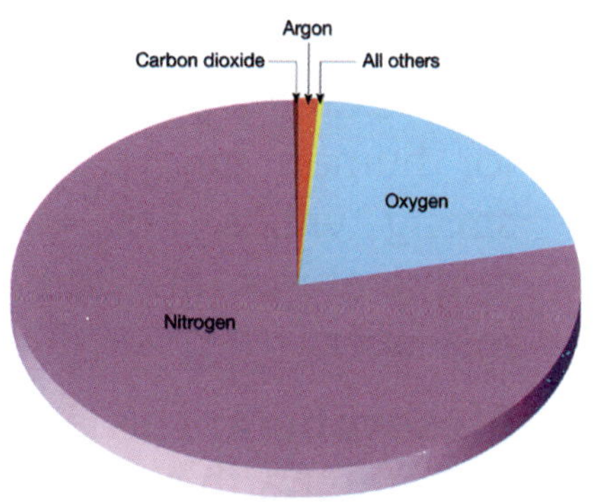

Gases in the Atmosphere

The 'Atmosphere' refers to the blanket of air that envelops the Earth. It consists of gases, particles and various other materials. The main component of the atmosphere is nitrogen which occupies around 78%, followed by oxygen that constitutes 21%. The rest 1% is made up of carbon dioxide and other materials that include minute particles of water vapour, methane, carbon monoxide, hydrogen, nitrous oxide, ozone, neon, helium, krypton nd xenon gases. In addition to these gases, the atmosphere consists of smoke, dust particles, volcanic ash, meteoric dust, pollen, etc.

The atmosphere is made up of many layers. The layers closer to the Earth's surface are denser than the ones away from it. The atmosphere extends up to 500 kilometers from the earth's surface and the pressure, temperature and density vary according to its height. The air pressure reduces to half as we ascend 6 kilometers from the Earth and the temperature falls by 1 degree Fahrenheit at the height of every 91 metres.

Based on its physical properties, the atmosphere has been divided into the following layers:

1. **Troposphere:** Occupies 75% of the total weight of the atmosphere, and extends up to 17 kilometers from the Earth's surface. It is the most essential layer of the atmosphere as all living beings live at this layer. Moreover, rain, clouds, storm, etc. are all formed in here.

2. **Stratosphere:** Extends till 48 kilometers, and the most important function of the stratosphere is that it absorbs the ozone rays radiated by the sun. These layers are extremely dangerous for human beings. Neither strong winds nor varying temperatures are found in this layer.

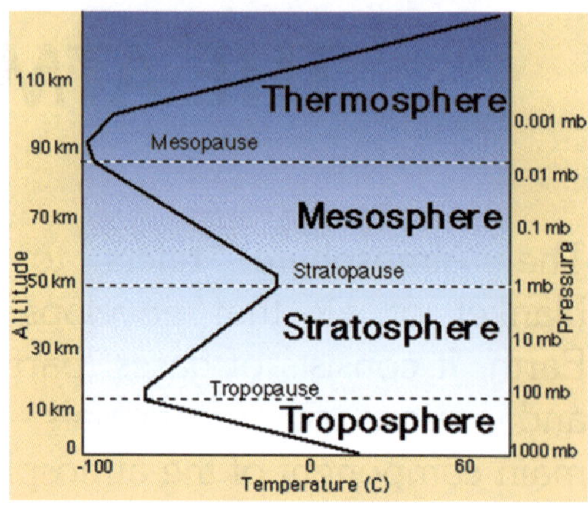

Layers of Atmosphere

3. **Mesosphere:** This layer begins from the height of 50 kilometers from the Earth's surface. The temperature in this layer is very low and it is the lowest at the height of 85 kilometers.

4. **Ionosphere:** Starts above the Mesosphere and extends up to 500 kilometers. This layer consists of charged particles that reflect radio waves towards the Earth and makes radio communication possible.

5. **Exosphere:** This is the outermost layer of the atmosphere, and the density here is very low. Due to the presence of helium and hydrogen, the chief components of this layer, the temperature is very high.

Actually, the atmosphere is extremely vital for our existence as it protects us from all the harmful radiations, meteors that come from the outer space.

Quick Facts

- The thermosphere is made of the ionosphere and magnetosphere. Here the air density is the lowest and this layer comprises just 0.001% of the total volume of atmospheric gases.
- In the ionosphere, sun radiations cause ionisation, i.e., the particles are electrically charged. The ionosphere reflects the radio waves employed in telecommunications.
- The magnetosphere is located above the ionosphere, at the external limit of the Earth's magnetic field. It behaves like a giant magnet, retaining high energy particles and thus protects the Earth. This layer has the lowest density.

Chapter - 2

AN APPLE A DAY KEEPS THE DOCTOR AWAY

There is an age-old saying, "An apple a day, keeps the doctor away." But is it actually true? Does an apple actually have the properties to keep all diseases at bay? The answer is NO.

Eating an Apple

This saying was just made as a polite way of making people realise that eating apples is a good habit as it prevents *constipation* and other related ailments. The juice of a raw apple is believed to help in the *fermentation of undigested food*.

Apple Juice

Though people of modern times find it arguable, it is unquestionable that an apple is good for health. An apple has high nutritive value due to which eating it is suggested as a habit one should develop, particularly the children and youngsters. Even older people can be benefitted by eating this fruit daily.

Some people have modified the saying as, "An apple a day, keeps the dentist away." This is so because it is believed that biting an apple helps remove the food particles lodged between the teeth effectively. It is said that eating an apple between meals and brushing our teeth in the morning and before retiring for the night is the best way to maintain oral health.

Eating an Apple

Due to its nutritional values, an apple is also believed to prevent diseases, such as *scurvy*, *night blindness*, etc. Since apples are rich in Vitamin A, C, cellulose and carbohydrates, they help in purifying blood, healing wounds, provide protection from cold. They also help in building strong bones, teeth and gums.

Eaten raw for taste and beneficial nutrients, an apple contains 80% water, while the remaining matter contains ascorbic acid (Vitamin C), sugar, other acids and rough indigestible matter.

Apart from being eaten raw, apples are also used to prepare sweet dishes such as apple pie. Cider is also brewed from fermented apples.

Apples are a member of the *Rosaceae* family. They are usually red, yellow, or green in colour in their ripened state. They grow in temperate zones in relatively cold weather.

Apple

By the end of 300 A.D., 37 varieties of apples were named by a Roman writer. However, in today's date, various varieties of apples are available, which differ in sweetness and flavour.

Quick Facts

- A fresh apple is an ideal, healthy snack for you because it's easy to carry, quite filling, juicy and refreshing. Some varieties provide you with a good source of Vitamin C, which is an antioxidant and helps to improve and maintain your immune system.
- Apples carry relatively low calories and contain high level of fructose. This natural sugar, although sweeter than sucrose (main component of cane sugar), gets metabolised slowly in the body, thereby it helps us to control our blood sugar levels.
- In herbal medicine, you'll see people using ripe, uncooked apples to treat constipation, while you can eat it stewed for treating diarrhoea and gastroenteritis. You can also use apples in poultices for skin inflammations.

Chapter - 3

WHY DO WE GET PINS AND NEEDLES?

The tingling sensation that we get in our hands, feet, arms, legs after they haven't been moved for some time is because the blood begins to circulate again in those parts of our body. In scientific terms, this sensation is called *Paresthesia*; however, it is generally referred to as *pins and needles*.

For example, after sitting for a long time with our legs crossed, we feel numbness when we try to stand up. We often refer to it as the legs 'falling asleep'. This happens due to the change when the blood begins to circulate in our legs again.

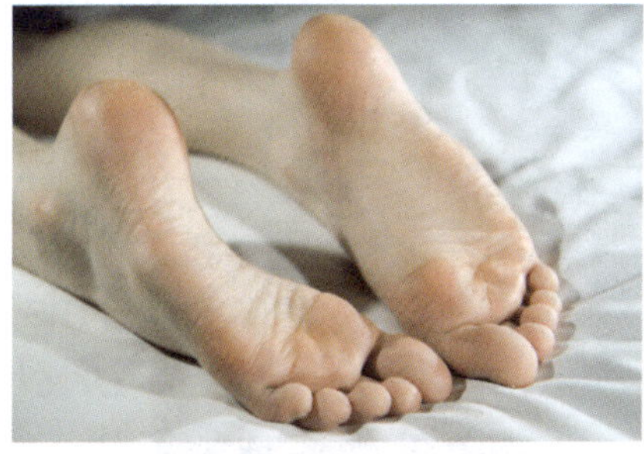

Feet

Have you ever wondered why we get this feeling? Let us try to understand this phenomenon through an easy example. It is a fact that blood circulates freely in our body, through blood vessels, such as arteries and veins just like water flows freely through a stretched water hose. Now imagine the hose is bent. What would happen? Obviously, the water would trickle through slowly.

Something similar happens in the case of the transportation of blood in our body. It has two main functions: (a) To supply food and oxygen to different parts of the body, and (b) To collect all the poisonous wastes. This flow is restricted if we block the path of our body parts for a long time. Due to this, the poisonous wastes get collected and this blocks the nerve cells from carrying any kind of messages from the affected body part to the brain. This leads to a feeling of numbness.

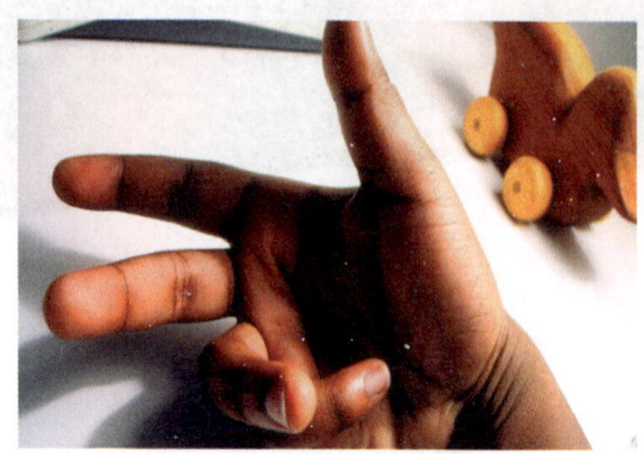

Paresthesia in Hands

When the body part is stretched after some time, there is a sudden rush of blood into the body part. Imagine this with the help of the water hose again. After bending the water hose, if it is stretched again, it is obvious that water would be allowed to flow freely again, causing a sudden rush in the water hose.

Exercise to Prevent Paresthesia

Similarly, when the transportation system of our body is released from the blockage, the blood begins to circulate freely again. It is this resumption of blood circulation that causes the *tingling sensation or pins and needles*.

This situation can be of two types, *transient or chronic*. *Transient paresthesia* is basically the numbness that we experience commonly. It is caused because of excessive pressure being applied on a nerve which leads to stopping its function temporarily. However, *chronic paresthesia* indicates a problem with the functioning of the neurons, which may require special medical attention.

Quick Facts

- Paresthesia sensations can be described in many different ways, including tingling, numbness, pins and needles, itching and burning. Paresthetic sensations may be accompanied by pain and other symptoms depending on the part of the body that is affected. Any associated symptoms can help your doctor make a diagnosis.
- Paresthesia usually arises from nerve compression (pressure or entrapment) or damage. Paresthesia can be a symptom of a wide variety of diseases, or disorders or due to injuries to the nerves.
- Temporary paresthesia can be due to any activity that causes prolonged pressure on a nerve or nerves such as sitting cross legged or bicycling a long distance. Paresthesia can also occur with moderate to severe orthopaedic conditions, as well as disorders and diseases that damage the nervous system.
- Because paresthesia can be due to a nervous system disease or nerve damage, failure to seek treatment can result in complications and permanent damage. The general symptoms are: Chronic pain, Inability to breathe on your own, Paralysis, Permanent loss of sensation.

Chapter - 4

THE CHANGE OF SEASONS

The Earth rotates on its own axis and revolves around the Sun also. *Day and night are caused due to the Earth's rotation around its axis* that makes a vertical angle of 23.5 degrees. It is because of this axis that as the Earth revolves around the Sun, its rays hit the Earth's surface at different angles and at different times of the year at one place.

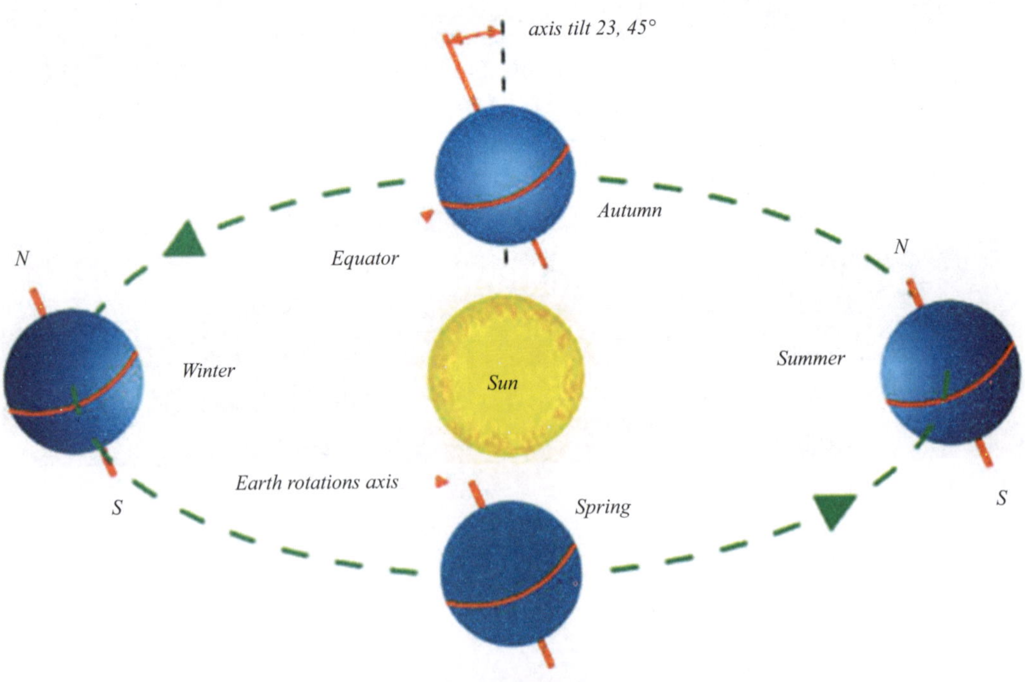

Formation of Different Seasons

Because of the variations in the angles, the solar heat gets distributed differently throughout the year at the same place. This uneven distribution of the solar heat causes the *change in seasons*.

Around June, the northern hemisphere is tilted towards the Sun and this causes summer in Europe, Asia and North America. Similarly, six months later, when the southern hemisphere is tilted towards the Sun, it experiences summer while the northern hemisphere experiences winter.

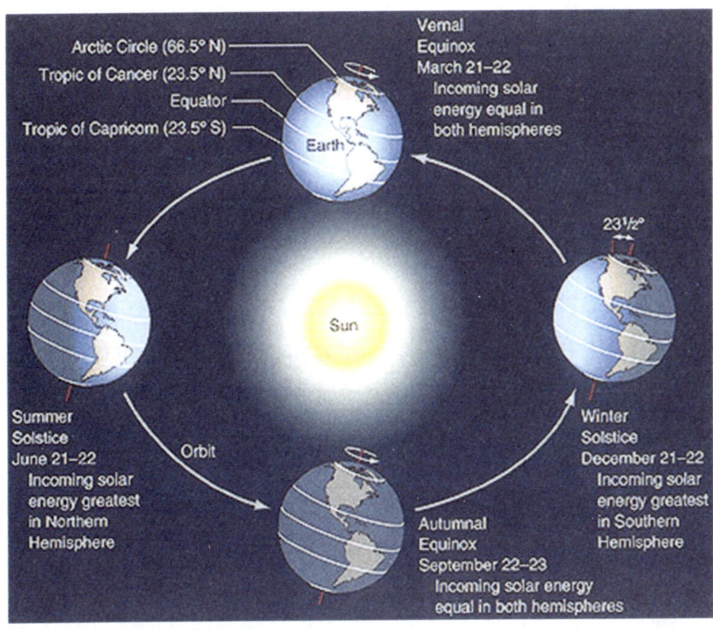

Summer Solstice, Winter Solstice and Equinoxes

March 21 and September 23 are two special dates as on these two days, the Sun is exactly over the Equator causing the duration of the day and night same (12 hours) at every place on the Earth. These dates are also called as **Equinoxes**. Between March 21 and June 21, the Sun advances towards the Tropic of Cancer, resulting in summer season in the northern hemisphere. This means longer days and shorter nights. It is during this time that the southern hemisphere experiences winters.

Globe showing the Tropic of Cancer

Between June 21 and December 22, the Sun moves towards the Tropic of

Capricorn, causing summers in the southern hemisphere and winters in the northern hemisphere. It is at this time that the northern hemisphere experiences shorter days and longer nights. After December 22, the Sun once again starts moving towards the north and reaches the equator on March 21. During this period, the days in the northern hemisphere once again start getting longer than the nights.

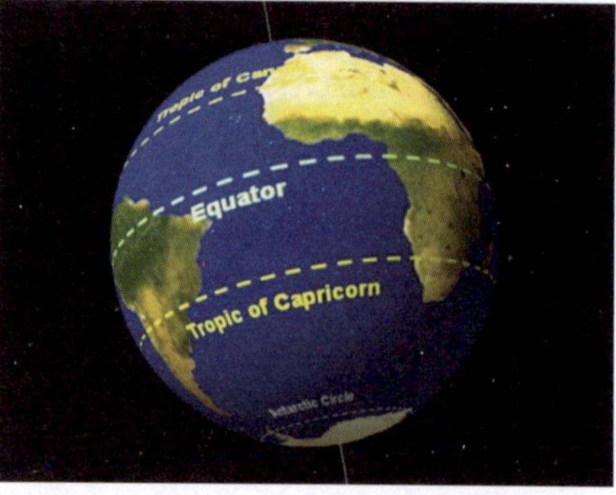

Globe Showing the Tropic of Capricorn

During the months of March and September, due to the Sun being overhead on the Equator, the hemispheres either experience *autumn or spring*.

It is thus the rotation of the Earth around its own inclined axis and its revolution around the Sun that causes the change in seasons from summer to winter in different hemispheres and also the transition from day to night.

Quick Facts

- **The seasons result from the Earth's axis being tilted to its orbital plane. Basically, the Earth's axis deviates by an angle of approximately 23.5 degrees. Thus, at any given time during summer or winter, one part of the planet is more directly exposed to the rays of the Sun. This exposure alternates as the Earth revolves in its orbit. Therefore, at any given time, regardless of season, the northern and southern hemispheres experience opposite seasons. This is known as the Axial Tilt.**
- **The effect of axial tilt is observable as the change in day time and altitude of the Sun at noon (the culmination of the Sun) during a year.**

- A season is a subdivision of the year, marked by changes in weather, ecology, and hours of daylight. Seasons result from yearly revolution of the Earth around the Sun and the tilt of the Earth's axis relative to the plane of revolution.
- In temperate and polar regions, the seasons are marked by changes in the intensity of sunlight that reaches the Earth's surface, variations of which may cause animals to go into hibernation or to migrate, and plants to be dormant.
- During May, June and July, the northern hemisphere is exposed to more direct sunlight because the hemisphere faces the sun. The same is true about the southern hemisphere in November, December and January. It is the tilt of the Earth that causes the Sun to be higher in the sky during the summer months which increases the solar flux. However, due to seasonal lag, June, July and August are the hottest months in the northern hemisphere and December, January and February are the hottest months in the southern hemisphere.

Chapter - 5

WHY DO PLANTS AND ANIMALS BECOME EXTINCT?

At the time Charles Darwin proposed his theory of, 'Survival of the Fittest', it entered into many controversies and received a lot of criticism. However, in due course of time, it started receiving wider acceptance as it was found that certain species were found to be either extinct or were facing extinction due to reasons explained by Darwin in his theory.

Charles Darwin

Since the time of evolution of animals and plants, many species have become entirely extinct. On the other hand,

Dinosaurs

certain species are facing the problem of becoming extinct. The conservation of these species has drawn alarming attention all over the world. Such species are called, the the '*endangered species*'.

Deforestation

The causes that have led certain species to become endangered are both natural and man-made. One of the primary reasons for this predicament is the ever-increasing human population. In order to fulfill their needs, human beings encroach upon more and more forest land, leading to scarcity of land for wildlife to survive.

Migration of Birds

To fulfill human needs, heaths and forests have been destructed to make farming space, large-scale wood is deforested and more and more industries are being set up. Due to these reasons, wildlife suffers a lot.

Monkey

Another reason for extinction is *hunting* and *poaching*. Man has hunted various species to extinction, the examples of which are the auk and dodo. Pollution is another factor that leads to this unpleasant phenomenon. Every year millions of birds die painful deaths because of withering feathers as they get covered by sticky black oil from oil spills.

Some natural factors such as unsuitable weather conditions, lack of food, natural calamities contribute to the *extinction of plants and animals*.

Leaves

Plants

Plants that need special measures of protection include helleborine, cheddar pink, monkey orchid, tufted saxifrage, alpine catchfly, and alpine gentian. On the other hand, animals facing extinction are elephants, tigers, lions, ocelot, humpbacks, whale, panda, leopard, rhinoceros, puma, polar bear, the giant sable antelope, etc.

The preservation of these species has drawn attention both at national and international levels. Effective measures are being taken to preserve wildlife such as, creation of *sanctuaries, implementation of stringent laws against poaching.*

Quick Facts

- **Plants can become endangered as many of the same ways animals become endangered. Although conservation attempts can be made to save the endangered plant species; help often comes too late.**
- **Many factors can cause a plant to become endangered. Many things that endanger animals, endanger plants too. The main cause of a plant species to become endangered is the loss of its natural habitat. This occurs because of the expansion of mankind. As the human population grows, the more land the mankind needs to survive comfortably. Unfortunately, as this improves the lives of humans, it threatens the survival of many plant species.**
- **Loss of natural plants habitats is also caused by an increase in wild fires. Over the years wild fires have began to intensify. Many believe wild fire is caused by global warming. As the temperatures rise the more wild fires appear. This causes many plant species to loose their natural habitat.**

- Other forces of nature can also threaten plant species. For example: Severe droughts can cause large numbers of plant species to die and possibly become extinct.
- Loss of a plant habitat also occurs due to the agricultural industry. As the need for more agriculture increases, the need for more land also increases. Land is often cleared to make pastures or crops. This causes plants to loose their habitat. Grazing animals can threaten many plant species as well.
- Plants can also become endangered by the intent of mankind. Many rare plants are often collected by mankind for their rare beauty. These valuable plants can often be found in florist shops and nurseries.
- When there are no more animals of a particular species left alive, that species is said to be extinct.

Chapter - 6

THE VISION OF OWLS

An Owl

An owl can rarely be seen during daytime. This is because while most birds are *diurnal* (active in daytime), owls are *nocturnal* creatures (active at night) that 'come to life' in the night. The physical features of an owl include a large head, big eyes, sharp claws, short neck and broad wings.

Around *130 species of owls* are known to us today. Some countries regard owls as auspicious creatures, while others consider them a symbol of *wealth and wisdom*.

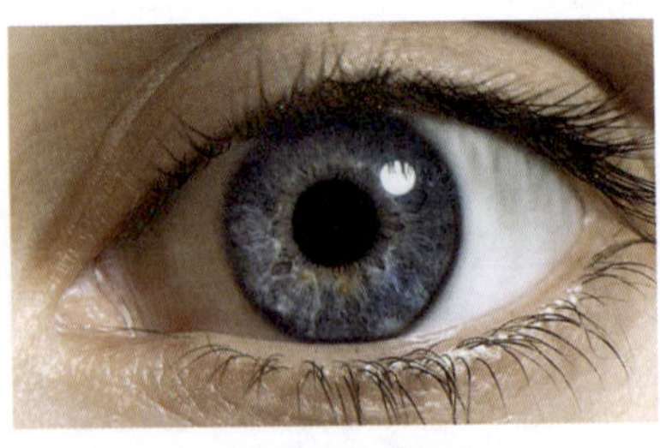

A Human Eye

The peculiar thing about owls is that while they *see clearer at night*, they have an *extraordinary sense of hearing during the day*. It is a matter of great curiosity to all as to how owls can see clearer at night than in the day.

Before we go ahead it is important to know how human beings see things. The light scattered by an object is focussed at our retina by the lenses inside the eyes. An inverted image is formed here which the optic nerves carry to the brain. The brain then inverts the image and we are able to see things.

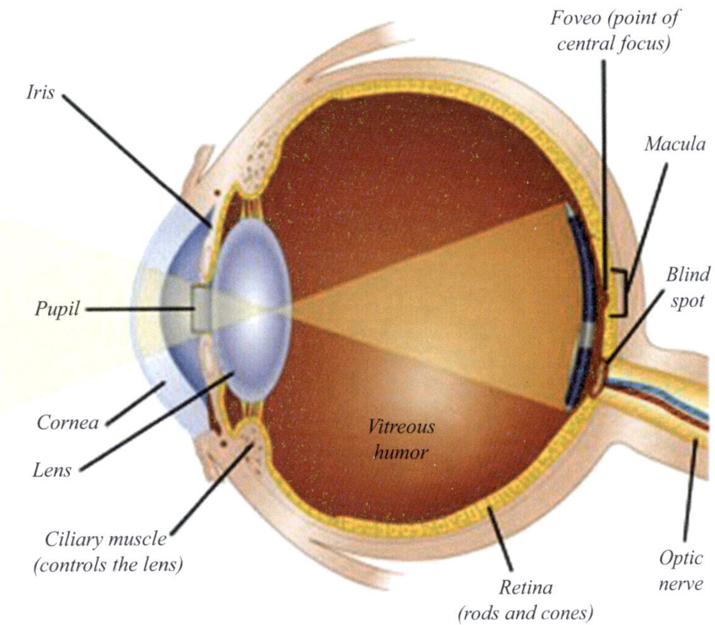

An Owl's Eye

The eyes of an owl are large and forward-pointed. There are four main reasons due to which owls are nocturnal.

Firstly, in the case of an owl, the distance between the retina and lens of the eye of an owl is more than that in human beings. This forms bigger images on the retina of the owl.

Secondly, an owl's retina has *10,000 rods and cones* per square millimetre compared to 2,000 in humans. This enables an owl to see five times more than us!

The third reason is a special red-coloured protein present in an owl's eyes, which makes its vision extremely sensitive to light. Thus, an owl is able to see things clearly, which others may find hazy.

The fourth reason for nocturnal nature of an owl is the fact that the pupil of the eye of an owl can dilate more, resulting in detecting the smallest amount of light.

Because of these four factors, an owl is more comfortable to watch things in the night. Due to these properties of its eyes, in daylight, objects appear extremely bright.

Another surprising thing about an owl is that it can rotate its head at an angle of 180 degrees, which is till the back of his head!

Quick Facts

- There are around 200 different species of owl.
- Owls are active at night (nocturnal).
- A group of owls is called a parliament.
- Most owls hunt insects, small mammals and other birds.
- Some owl species hunt fish.
- Owls have powerful talons (claws) which help them catch and kill prey.
- Owls have large eyes and a flat face.
- Owls can turn their heads as much as 270 degrees.
- Owls are farsighted, i.e. they can't see things close to their eyes clearly.
- Owls are very quiet in flight compared to other birds of prey.
- The colour of owl's feathers helps them blend into their environment (camouflage), which also helps them to catch their prey.
- Barn owls can be recognised by their heart shaped face.

Chapter - 7

THE MAP OF MIGRATORY BIRDS

Migratory Birds

Every year, in the months of spring, millions of birds migrate from colder to temperate regions of the world in order to breed. Basically, they migrate to different places to have abundance of food for them to rear their chicks.

Birds need to adjust their metabolic systems to meet the needs of the migration process. Energy storage through fat accumulation and sleep control in nocturnal migrants require special physiological adaptations. Moreover, the feathers of a bird suffer from wear and tear and need to be moulted. Apart from this, migration also requires changes in behavioural patterns such as flying in flocks to reduce the energy used or risk of predation during migration.

The northern parts of North America, Europe, and Asia receive the maximum number of migrations. The southern hemisphere also gets migratory birds like the Double Banded Dotted Plover bird flies from Australia to New Zealand to breed. Wild Geese fly north in the northern hemisphere during spring and in autumn, they fly south to

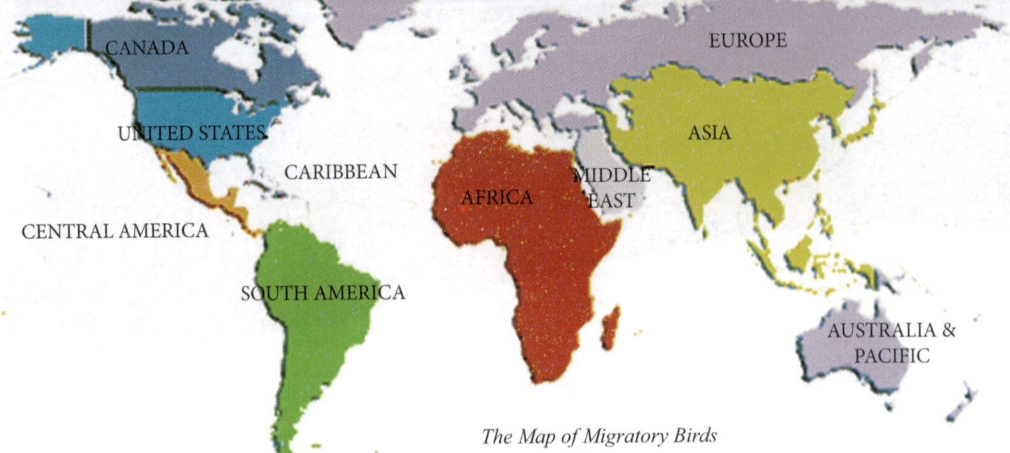

The Map of Migratory Birds

breed, while the American Gold Plover flies about 3325 kilometers non-stop from Alaska to Hawaii.

The main cause behind migration is the change in the length of the day due to changing seasons which ultimately change the birds' hormonal balance.

Bats

One may often wonder how exactly a bird is able to find its way from its home region to the migratory place and back. Well, the answer to this query is the proof of a bird's intelligence.

Like in any other structure where the young ones learn and follow the old and experienced, even birds follow this principle of migration.

Young birds that are migrating for the first time fly with the older ones who have taken the trip before and guide them through the migration route.

While flying, birds make note of landmarks such as lakes, mountains, coastlines, etc., to remember their route of migration. Some birds are even intelligent enough to use the sun and stars to navigate to and fro from the migrating region.

Eels

Birds are not the only species that migrate. Many other animals such as mammals, flying insects, fish, locusts, eels, etc., also migrate in order to survive bad weather and breeding problems.

Quick Facts

- The word, 'migration' comes from the Latin word, migratus that means 'to change' and refers to how birds change their geographic locations seasonally.
- Migration peaks in spring and fall, but in reality, there are birds migrating 365 days a year. The actual dates when birds migrate depends on many factors, including bird species, migration distance, travel speed, route, climate and more.
- Before migrating, many birds enter a state of hyperphagia, where hormone levels compel them to drastically increase their body weight and store fat to use as energy while travelling. Some bird species may as much as double their body weight in the weeks leading up to migration.
- Birds may fly from 15-600 miles or more per day during migration, depending on when they are migrating, how far they have to go and the conditions they face along the route, including the availability of suitable stopovers.
- Hawks, swifts, swallows and waterfowl migrate primarily during the day, while many songbirds migrate at night, in parts to avoid the attention of migrating predators such as the raptors. The cooler, calmer air at night also makes migration more efficient for many species, while those that migrate during the day most often take advantage of the solar-heated thermal currents for easy soaring.
- Migrating birds use the stars for navigation, as well as the sun, wind patterns and landforms, all of these help them to guide the same locations, each year. The earth's magnetic field also plays a part in how birds migrate.

Chapter - 8

THE COLOUR OF FIREWORKS

Fireworks, often known as fire crackers, are used to celebrate various occasions of happiness such as weddings, festivals. Once lighted, they explode and burst into a variety of colours, because of which they remain a special attraction amongst children. Over 300 varieties of fireworks are available in markets and it is approximated that a sum of Rupees 5,000 crore is spent on the purchase of crackers, every year.

The Colour of Fireworks

People enjoy bursting crackers and looking at the colourful explosions. However, have you ever wondered where the colours in the fireworks come from? The answer to this question lies in the ambit of science.

Fireworks are made from a mixture of potassium nitrate, sulphur, coal, and certain other metal salts. In addition to these, chemicals like strontium, barium, magnesium and sodium that add colour to the fireworks are used. These are combined with potassium chlorate.

The green colour in the fireworks is due to the presence of barium salts, while the production of light blue colour is because of strontium sulphate. The yellow colour is produced by strontium carbonate whereas strontium nitrate gives red colour. Apart from these, salts of sodium impart shades of yellow, while those of copper are responsible for the production of yellow hues. The silvery rain from the fireworks comes from the presence of aluminium powder.

Fireworks during Diwali

At the time of explosion, the salts present in the fireworks burn to produce various colours, creating a beautiful and colourful view.

Fireworks were first manufactured in China thousands of years ago. The trend was shortly followed by various regions of Europe, Arabia, and Greece. Today the largest firework manufacturer of the world is a small town named Sivaski, located in the south of India.

However, we must realise that the bursting of crackers causes harm to the environment. Fireworks cause great amount of pollution which often mixes up with fog in the winter and creates smog which is harmful for plants. Moreover, a large number of trees are destroyed for the production of crackers. Hence, we should burn fireworks as less as possible.

Map of World

Quick Facts

- Creating firework colours is a complex endeavour, and requires considerable art and application of physical science. Excluding propellants or special effects, the points of light ejected from fireworks, termed as 'stars', generally require an oxygen-producer, fuel, binder (to keep everything where it needs to be), and colour producer. There are two main mechanisms of colour production in fireworks, *incandescence and luminescence.*
- Incandescence is light produced from heat. Heat causes a substance to become hot and glow, initially emitting infrared, then red, orange, yellow, and white light as it becomes increasingly hotter. When the temperature of a firework is controlled, the glow of components, such as charcoal, can be manipulated to be the desired colour (temperature) at proper time. Metals, such as aluminum, magnesium and titanium, burn very brightly and are useful for increasing the temperature of the fireworks.
- Luminescence is light produced using energy sources other than heat. To produce luminescence, energy is absorbed by an electron of an atom or molecule, causing it to become excited but unstable. When the electron returns to a lower energy state, the energy is released in the form of a photon (light). The energy of the photon determines its wavelength or colour.
- Sometimes the salts needed to produce the desired

colour are unstable. Barium chloride (green) is unstable at room temperatures, so barium must be combined with a more stable compound (e.g., chlorinated rubber).

- Copper chloride (blue), which is present in fireworks is unstable at high temperatures, so the firework cannot get too hot, yet must be bright enough to be seen.

Chapter - 9

THE FORMATION OF A RAINBOW

Rainbows give a beautiful look of colours in nature. After rains, rainbows spread a breeze of cheer and happiness into the hearts of its viewers. A rainbow appears when the sun shines through the rain.

Formation of Rainbow

Though sunlight appears white, it consists of seven different shades, namely, *violet, indigo, blue, green, yellow, orange, and red*, abbreviated as VIBGYOR. When sunlight splits into seven colours, the process is called *dispersion*, while the strip of seven colours is referred to as a **spectrum**.

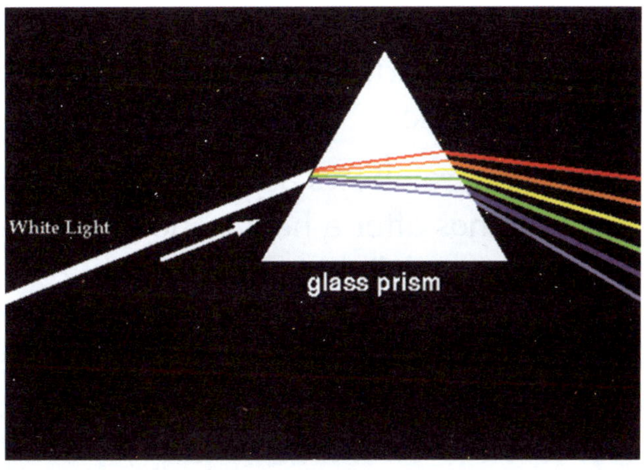

The Spectrum of Light

A rainbow usually appears after rain when tiny drops of water fill the atmosphere. When sunrays fall on these spherical water droplets, they act like prisms. This results in the rays getting refracted and split up into the **VIBGYOR** colours as they pass through the raindrops.

Since each ray of light gets refracted in a different angle from the prism, they separate into seven different colours, forming a **Rainbow**. It also thus proves that white light is made up of seven colours.

The shape of a rainbow is that of a semi-circular arc. This is because the sun is circular. A rainbow is called complete when it has both a primary and a secondary arc. The primary arc has violet on the inner side, followed by indigo, blue, green, yellow, orange and red. In the secondary arc, the order of the colours is reversed. Red colour is on the inner side, while violet is on the outermost.

In a complete rainbow, the location of the secondary arc is above the primary arc. This kind of a rainbow is formed when the sun's rays are reflected and refracted after the first reflection and refraction within the same raindrop.

A rainbow always appears in the opposite direction from the sun.

For the formation of a rainbow the sun shine just after the rain. It is extremely important for our eyes that the sun and the rainbow lie in the same plane.

Most often, rainbows are formed and seen in the early mornings or late evenings after a heavy shower. A beautiful and vibrant sight of rainbows is a delight to the eyes.

Quick Facts

- **A rainbow can be defined as a band of colours (from red on the inside to violet on the outside) assembled as an arc that is formed by reflection and refraction (or bending) of the sun's rays inside raindrops. They appear when it is raining in one part of the sky and is sunny in another.**
- **Most people think the only colours of a rainbow are red, orange, yellow, green, blue, indigo and violet, popularly abbreviated as VIBGYOR but a rainbow is actually made up of an entire continuum of colours—even colours the eye can't see!**
- **We are able to see the colours of a rainbow because the light of different colours is refracted when it travels from one medium, such as air, into another- in this case, the water of the raindrops. When all the colours that make up sunlight are combined, they look white, but once they are refracted, the colours break up into the ones we see in a rainbow.**

Chapter - 10

WHAT IS MILK MADE UP OF?

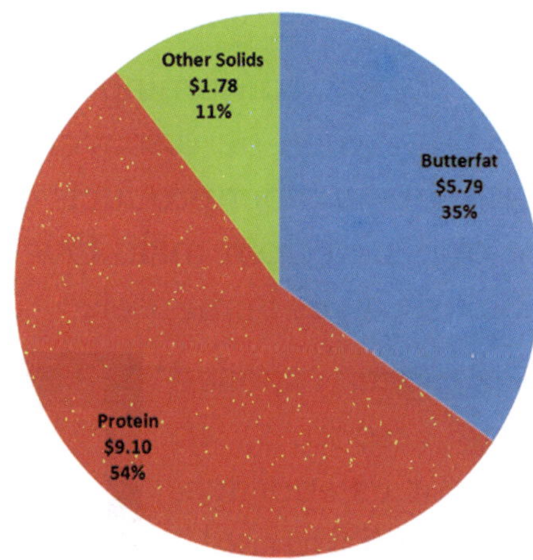

Essential Components in Milk

One often wonders why mothers keep asking their children to have milk every day. Some children love milk but others don't. There is an adequate percentage of nutrients a glass of milk contains; that is why milk cannot be substituted by their favourite aerated drink. Given below are many reasons for the same.

Milk is highly nutritious, i.e., the white liquid produced by mammals to feed their young ones. Usually the milk obtained from cows and buffaloes is used by human beings. However, in many other parts of the world, milk is obtained from other animals as well. For example, people in northern Europe consume reindeer's milk and those in the Middle East countries consume goat's milk.

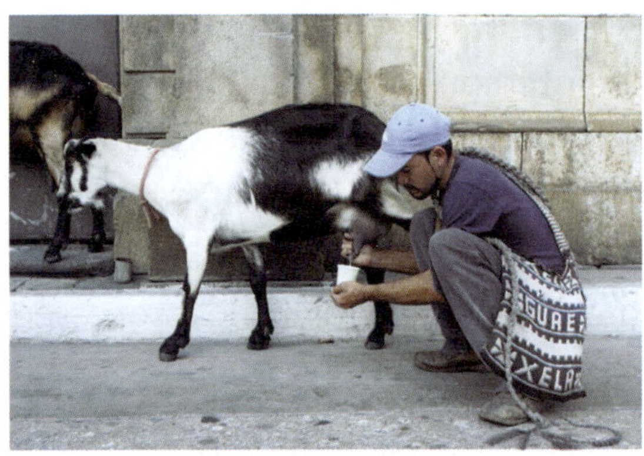
A Man Milking a Goat

Milk is often known as the "complete food". This is so because it has all the vital nutrients to ensure our good health. Cow's milk constitutes 87.2% water, 3.5% proteins, 3.7% fat, and 4.9% sugar among other vitamins and minerals. Different animals have these nutrients too, but in different proportions.

Different nutrients have different qualities. While proteins present in the milk help us to grow and enhance our physical strength, sugar acts as a fuel, and fats give us extra energy. Milk also contains minerals like calcium and phosphorus which help in bone formation. Besides that, vitamins **A, B, C, D, E, K,** and niacin present in milk help reduce vitamin deficiency for healthier growth.

Man started consuming milk over 5,000 years ago and this was the time when he discovered its various uses. Apart from its pure form, many other products of milk, such as *curd, butter, cheese* can be obtained from milk. Over time, these products are used in our domestic lives immensely.

Milk Products

Milk gets spoiled very soon. To prevent its spoilage, it is essential to cool it to 10 degrees celsius within 2 hours from milking and should be maintained at that temperature at the time of transportation from the source to the destination.

It is advisable to boil milk once before consuming it. This is called pasteurisation. It is done in order to control and stop the growth of micro bacteria in the milk. However, boiling it several times in a day kills its nutrients.

In recent times, many people have begun preferring processed milk due to health reasons. The consumption of homogenised and skimmed milk is rising because, through these processes, the fat in the milk is reduced or completely removed.

Quick Facts

- Milk is a white liquid produced by the mammary glands of mammals. It is the primary source of nutrition for young mammals before they are able to digest other types of food. Early-lactation milk contains colostrum, which carries the mother's antibodies to the baby and can reduce the risk of many diseases in the baby. It also contains many other nutrients.
- Milk is basically an emulsion of butterfat globules within a water-based fluid that contains dissolved carbohydrates and protein aggregates with minerals.
- As an agricultural product, milk is extracted from mammals and used as food for humans. In the year, 2011, worldwide dairy farms produced about 730 million tonnes of milk.
- India is the world's largest producer and consumer of milk, yet it neither exports nor imports milk. New Zealand, the European Union's 27 member states, Australia, and the United States are the world's largest exporters of milk and milk products. China and Russia are the world's largest importers of milk and milk products.

Chapter - 11

TELESCOPES

An optical instrument called a telescope is a tube-like tool used to see distant objects with magnified clarity.

It was invented in 1608 by Hans Lippershey, a Dutch optician. The following year, Galileo made his first telescope with a magnification of thirty. This made him observe the rings of Saturn and the moons of Jupiter.

Hans Lippershey

Galileo Galilei

Today, mainly three kinds of telescopes exist:

(i) Refracting telescopes

(ii) Reflecting telescopes

(iii) Radio telescopes

People also use binoculars to observe carefully the distant objects, which are basically two telescopes joined together to watch mountain peaks, horse races.

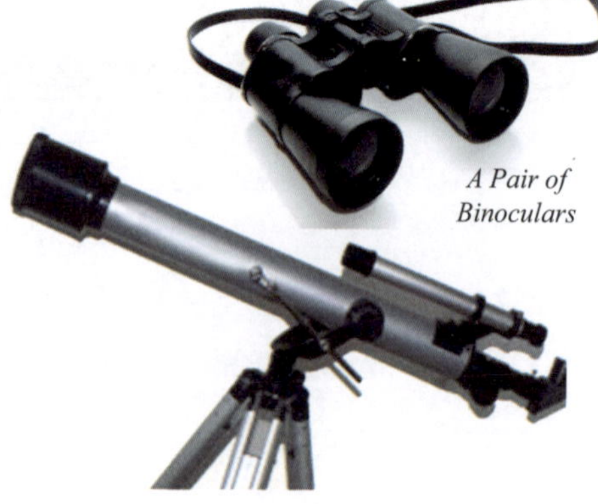

A Pair of Binoculars

Refracting Telescope

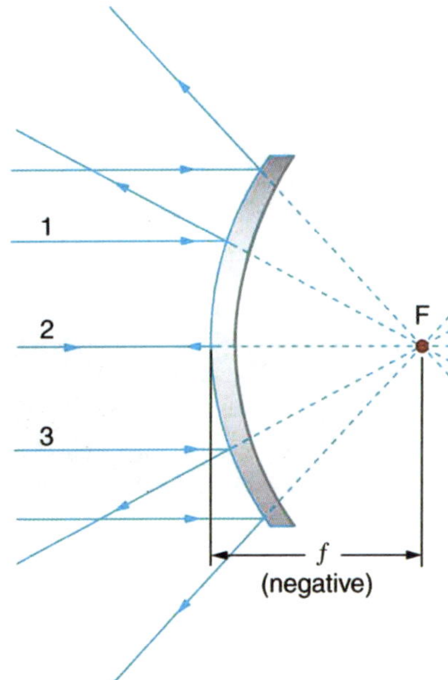

A Convex Mirror with Light Reflecting from it

A **Refracting Telescope** uses its lenses to bend or refract light. It makes use of two lenses fitted together. A larger sized convex objective lens and a convex eye piece is used in an astronomical telescope. However, a **Galilean Telescope** uses a convex lens and a concave eye piece.

Modern-day Refracting Telescopes are much more advanced.

This kind of a telescope is made of a concave mirror that gathers and focusses light rays. It also has a mirror near the point, where the light rays come together. It reflects back the rays into the eye piece.

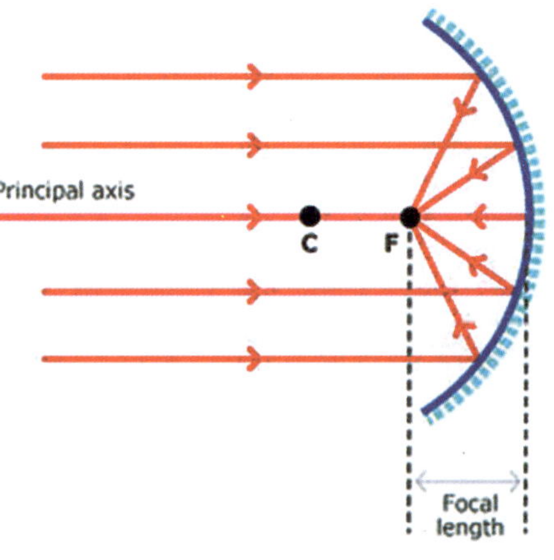

A Concave Mirror with Light Reflecting from it

Radio Telescope

The **Newtonian Telescope** uses a mirror set at an angle of 45 degrees to reflect light into the eye piece.

A **Schmidt – Cassegrain Telescope** has a convex lens. It reflects light into a tiny hole in the centre of the objective mirror.

Radio Telescopes were invented in 1930s. Usually, they contain a dish-shaped radio wave collector. They can see through the clouds and can be used at any time of the day as their work is based on radio waves rather than light.

The largest radio dish collector in the world is of 305 metres in diameter.

Reflecting Telescope

Quick Facts

- **Dutchman Hans Lippershey invented the telescope in 1608, but the legend is that the device was really invented three years earlier by kids playing with lenses in a spectacle-maker's shop.**
- **Telescopes gave rise to the first high-speed telecommunication networks: spyglasses that were used to relay semaphore signals from miles away.**
- **Galileo was the first to turn the telescope skyward, leading to the discovery of Jupiter's satellites and craters on the moon. He also pointed his telescope at the sun, which may have triggered his later blindness.**
- **Ireland's "Leviathan of Parsonstown," a 40-ton reflecting telescope built by the Earl of Rosse in 1845, was the world's largest for seven decades. But wet weather kept it shut down most of the time.**

- To deliver the 100-inch mirror for the Hooker Telescope on Mount Wilson in California, nearly 200 men with ropes guided a truck along a tortuous, eight-hour drive to the top but it was worth it. The Hooker Telescope proved that other galaxies exist and that the universe is expanding.
- Today, using an Internet-based Telescope such as the Seeing in the Dark scope at New Mexico Skies, any amateur can command a robotic observatory while lounging at home. Most professional astronomers now work that way too, and operate telescopes remotely with computers and rarely looking through an eyepiece.
- The NASA or the National Aeronautics and Space Administration is the agency of the United States government that is responsible for the nation's civilian space program and for aeronautics and aerospace research. Since February 2006, the NASA's mission statement has been to "pioneer the future in space exploration, scientific discovery and aeronautics research." The NASA launched the Hubble Space Telescope in 1990, seven years later with a budget of over $ 2 million.

Chapter - 12

WHY ARE SOME STARS BIGGER THAN THE OTHERS?

While gazing at the night sky, one can easily observe that some stars appear bigger than others. While looking at the stars through a telescope, one can spot differences in the brightness and colour of various stars.

Stars in the Night Sky

Have you ever wondered why this is so? The features of a star are very mysterious. Stars are never constant and change depending upon many factors.

The temperature of a star determines its colour and brightness. If the temperature of the star is high, its brightness increases. The brightness of a star depends on the relationship between its colour and temperature. Together, these two factors determine if the star would shine bright or not. Stars that appear red or yellow have the lowest surface temperature. Stars that are yellow or green have a slightly higher temperature. These are followed by white-coloured stars. Stars that appear blue have the highest surface temperature.

The temperature of the stars that are blue in colour can be as high as 27,750 degrees celsius. The Sun is a yellow star. Knowing this, we can just imagine how much hotter a blue star can be.

The typical temperature of a yellow star is about 6,000 degrees celsius. Stars that appear red or fainter yellow are

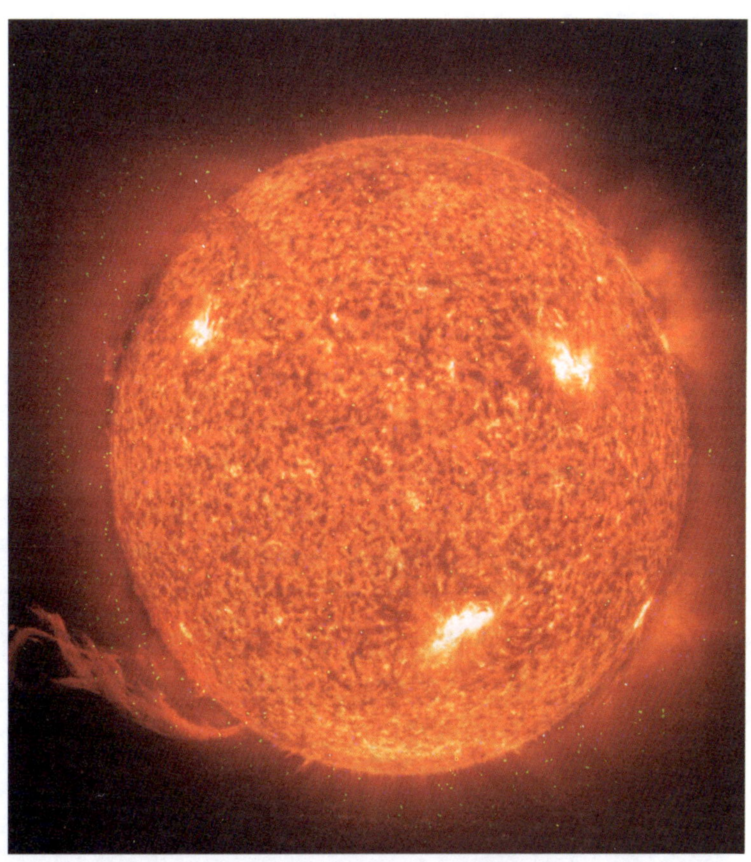

The Sun

comparatively cooler, with an approximate temperature of 1,650 degrees celsius. The above mentioned facts imply that the brightness of stars is directly related to the temperature of their surface.

Apart from this, another factor that determines the brightness of a star is its distance from us. If the star is farther away, it appears *fainter*, whereas a star close to the Earth shines *bright*.

It can also happen that stars that are much brighter than others due to their surface temperature may not shine distinctly in the night sky because their distance from our planet is enormous.

This situation is comparable to that of street lamps. The lamps that are closer to our vision appear brighter than the ones that are away from us.

Quick Facts

- **Stars are all made up of matter...so this question could be addressed as; how do forming stars obtain more matter?. The answer is simply more gravity. Gravity is defined as the force of attraction between two masses. As the star attracts more matter, its gravity increases and this process of attracting matter speeds up.**
- **The only way gravity can increase is if there is plenty of matter available. Matter isn't spread out uniformly across the universe and often, it's clustered in vast 'pockets' of gases and particles called 'Nebulae'.**
- **Nebulae are where stars are born. If a star is forming inside a particular large Nebula, it has more matter available, and therefore, the stars' gravity can continue to grow and create a larger star than a star in a Nebula with less matter.**

However, the above reason is certainly not the only reason how the size of a star varies, but is the easiest way to explain. It's also easier to understand that the Sun was created inside the same Nebula as other local stars, which is why we don't find particularly larger stars close to the Earth; which is probably a good thing.

Chapter - 13

WHO MEASURED THE UNIVERSE?

One may often wonder if it is possible for the universe to be measured. The universe consists of not only the Earth and the Solar System, but also stars, galaxies. Considering these facts, it may seem impossible to have an exact measurement of the universe.

The universe is beyond imagination. It is impossible for a layman to think about estimating the measure of the universe. Over time,

The Universe

many scientists and astronomers have attempted to solve this huge task but it continued to stay a riddle for a long time.

This scientific breakthrough was made by American astronomer, **Edwin Hubble**. He was the first scientist to successfully measure distances beyond our galaxy, the *Milky Way* or the *'Akash Ganga'* as it is called in the Indian Astronomy.

Edwin Powell Hubble

Edwin Hubble came up with various theories. One of them was the **Hubble's Law** which states that the distant galaxies are receding from each other at greater speed than the galaxies closer to ours.

He used the largest telescope available (2.5 metres, on Mount Wilson, California) and tried measuring the universe. He succeeded in measuring the distance of stars in the **Andromeda Galaxy**. He did so by measuring the brightness of the stars. Through this, he could judge how far the stars were from each other. Due to doubts about the brightness of the stars, he obtained a result of about 8,00,000 light years. At present, it is about two million light years away.

If we go by the Hubble's Law, the speed of galaxies is proportional to the distance between them. This represents the modern day picture of Cosmology. It suggests that all galaxies were once very close to each other and it was only in time that they receded from each other. This concept even supports the **Big Bang Theory** which talks about similar things.

Walter Buade

The actual measurement of the universe did not come forth till a long time. It was only around the time of World War II that the renowned astronomer, **Walter Buade** was able to determine the actual measurement of galactic distances. His observations proved Edwin Hubble wrong. It came out that the universe was much larger than what Hubble had estimated.

Quick Facts

- **The top ranked scientific justification for building the Hubble Telescope was to determine the size and age of the Universe through observations of Cepheid variables in distant galaxies. This scientific goal was so important that it put constraints on the lower limit of the size of Hubble's primary mirror.**
- **Cepheids are a special type of variable stars with very stable and predictable brightness variations. The period of these variations depends on the physical properties of the stars, such as their mass and true brightness. This means that astronomers, just by looking at the variability of their light, can find out about the Cepheids' physical nature, which then can be used very effectively to determine their distances. For this reason, cosmologists call Cepheids as 'standard candles'.**
- **Astronomers have used the Hubble Telescopes to observe Cepheids with extraordinary results. The Cepheids have then been used as stepping-stones to make distance measurements for supernovae, which have, in turn, given a measure for the scale of the Universe. Today, we know the age of the Universe to a much higher precision than before.**

Chapter - 14

HOW ARE DATES DETERMINED?

Over time, man has realised that stars are not mere objects to look at and admire. There are innumerable stars in the sky and since times immemorial they have helped man in various ways.

The pole star is known as a guiding star as it leads man to his bearings. Concepts like astronomy have emerged from the study of these tiny sparkles in the sky. Man has always been fascinated with stars and has hence invented powerful telescopes to study them. In time, he has been able to extract valuable information about stars.

One of the many wonderful things about stars is that one can determine dates with their help. In order to understand how, we have to undertake an activity.

The Pole Star

In order to determine the date, make a circle of at least 8 inches diameter on a large sheet of paper. Then, divide the circle into 12 equal parts, in the same way a clock face is divided.

Now, write the name of each month on each division of the paper. At the position of 12 o' clock, write the month, March and following the usual order of months, list them anti-clockwise.

Locate the centre of the circle and mark it as the 'North Star'. Now, imagine the distance between every month on the circle which is further divided into 30 parts.

Next, take the sheet of paper out on a clear night and hold it in such a way that March is on the top. Visualise the diagram in the night sky with the **North Star** in the centre. Take note of the location of the **Bid Dipper** and draw it on the diagram in the same way you find it in the sky. After this, draw a straight line from the pointer to the North Star. The line drawn will pass through the circle at a point which will indicate the date of when the observation has been taken.

For example, if the line passes between June and July, it is the 15th of June. It is important to draw a large circle, or else, it would be difficult to find the exact date. One can only come near the actual date.

The vital part is to remember that on the diagram, if an observation is made at midnight on a particular date, the pointers should be in the line with that date on the star calendar. This is the way of finding the date with the help of stars.

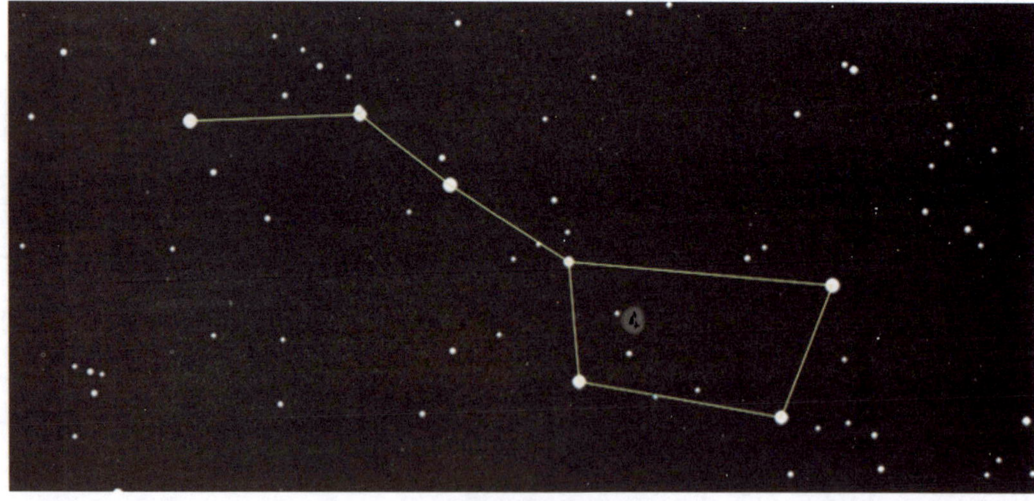

The Big Dipper

Quick Facts

- The Gregorian Calendar is today's internationally accepted civil calendar and is also known as the 'Western Calendar' or the 'Christian Calendar'. It was named after the man who first introduced it in February 1582 called Pope Gregory XIII.
- The calendar is strictly a *solar calendar* based on a 365-day common year divided into 12 months of irregular lengths. Each month consists of either 30 or 31 days with 1 month consisting of 28 days during the common year. A Leap Year usually occurs after every 4 years which adds an extra day to make the second month of February, 29 days long rather than 28 days.
- The *Gregorian Calendar* reformed the *Julian Calendar* because the Julian Calendar introduced an error of 1 day, every 128 years. However, a number of days had to be dropped when the change was made.
- The Gregorian Calendar was first adopted in Italy, Poland, Portugal and Spain in 1582.
- The rule for calculating Leap Years was changed to include that a year is a Leap Year if:

  a) The year is evenly divisible by 4.

  b) If the year can be evenly divided by 100, it is NOT a leap year, unless the year is also evenly divisible by 400.

  Simply put, any year evenly divisible by 4 or 400 (end of century) is a Leap Year.

Chapter - 15

WHY DON'T WE FEEL THE EARTH'S MOTION?

Earlier, it was believed that the Earth was the centre of the universe and all objects, the Sun, the Moon, and other Planets revolved around it. This assumption was based on the fact that the Earth was stationary while the placement of the stars and planets seemed to change over time.

The Planet, Earth

The breakthrough to this false belief came when **Nicholas Copernicus**, a Polish astronomer, who put forth his theory of the Earth's revolution around the Sun.

Nicholas Copernicus

It was hence proved that the Earth revolves around the Sun and completes one full revolution in *365 and one-fourth days*. This is the *period of one year according to the calendar*.

Also, it was proved that the Earth rotates along its own axis which makes a *vertical angle of 23 and half degrees*. One rotation gets completed in *24 hours and this makes one full day*.

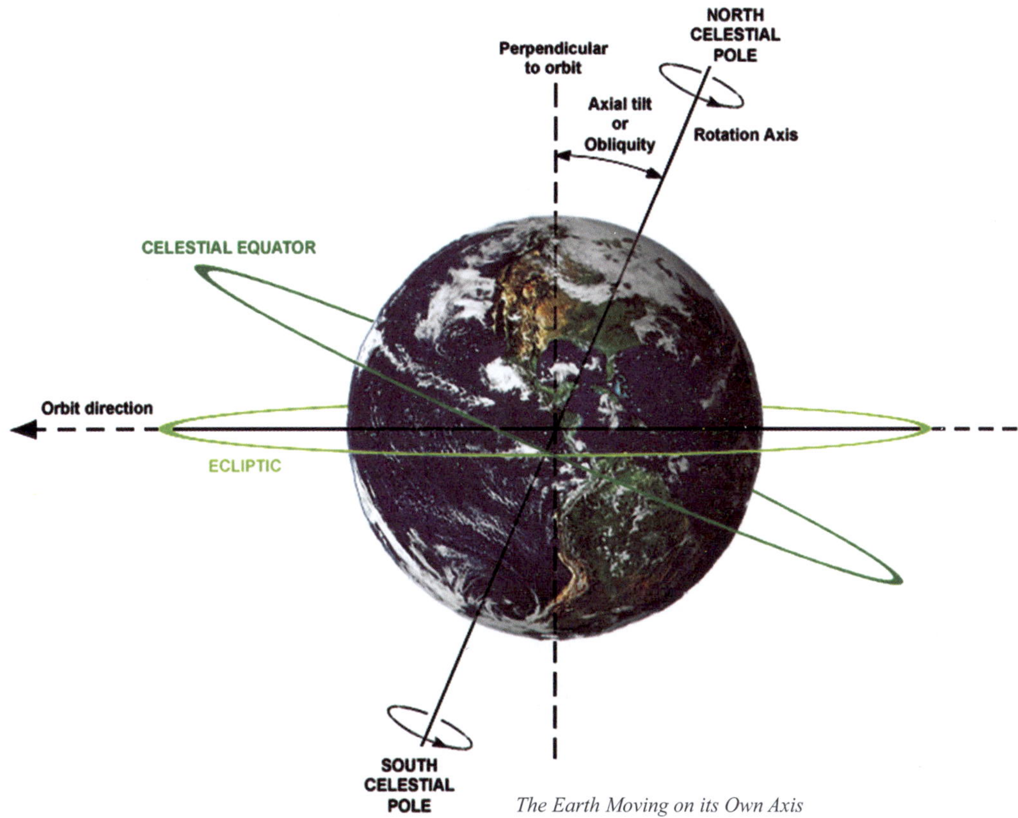

The Earth Moving on its Own Axis

The question that arises is, if the *Earth rotates and revolves at the same* time, why do'nt we feel any motion? It is because of the force of gravity. All things on this Earth move along with it and hence, we don't feel it.

It is like an ant on a rotating football. The ant doesn't feel any movement because it moves with the ball. Similarly, all objects on the Earth move along with it. Hence, we are unable to feel any kind of motion of the Earth as it rotates or revolves.

The *change of seasons* is the biggest proof of the Earth's motion. The seasons change because of the *Earth's revolution* around the

Sun and because of its *rotation along its own axis*. Day and night are caused because of rotation as the part of the Earth that faces the Sun *experiences day* while the *other experiences night*.

If the Earth did not rotate, the part facing the Sun would always get day, while the other would experience night all the time. The Earth's axis makes a vertical angle of 23 and half degrees. As a result of this, the North Pole and the South Pole faces the Sun for six continuous months. This explains the six-month duration of days and nights at the poles.

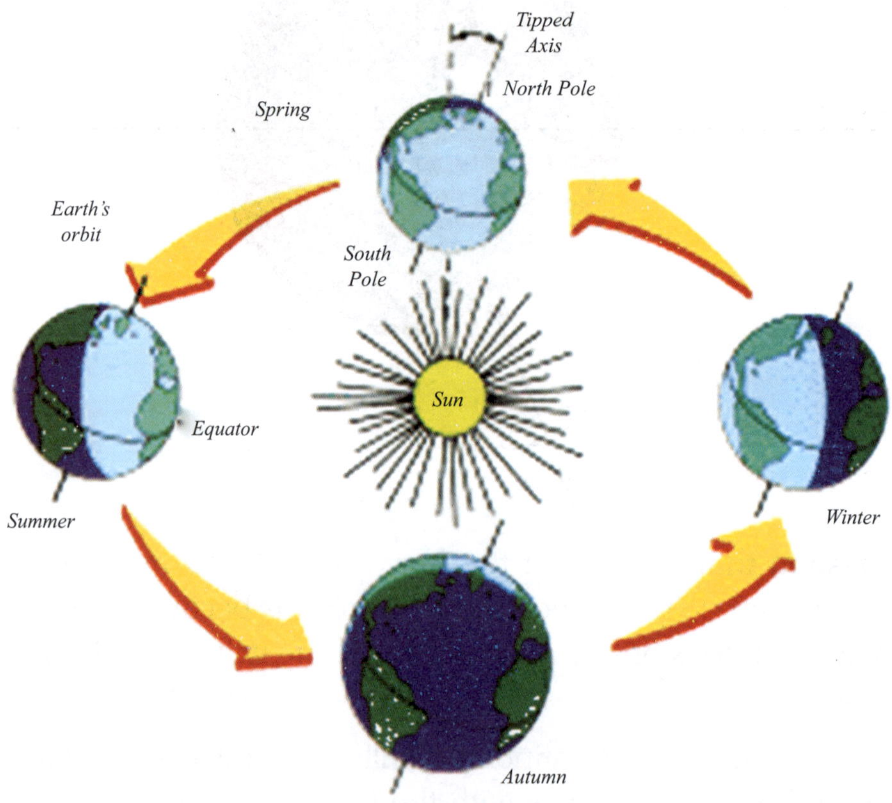

Sunlight Hitting Different Parts of the Earth

The day and night are caused by the Earth's rotation, while the change of seasons occurs due to its revolution around the Sun.

Quick Facts

- We don't feel the Earth spin because along with us, the atmosphere, skyscrapers, and everything else are spinning along at the same constant speed.
- The Earth's spin the same sensation as when you're travelling in a car or flying in a plane. A jumbo jet flies at about 500 miles per hour – that's about 800 kilometers an hour – about half as fast as the Earth spins at its Equator. But if you close your eyes, you don't feel like you're moving at all. And when the flight attendant comes by and pours coffee into your cup, the coffee doesn't fly to the back of the aeroplane. That's because the coffee, the cup and you are all moving at the same speed as the plane.
- Likewise, the Earth is moving at a fixed rate – and we're all moving along with it. Now imagine being on the jumbo jet again – think about what happens when the pilot suddenly speeds up or slows down the plane. You sometimes sense this change as a feeling of being pushed into your seat. In the same way, if the Earth were suddenly to speed up or slow down, you would definitely feel it.
- But as long as the Earth spins steadily and moves at a constant rate in orbit around the Sun – you as an Earthly passenger move right along with it.
- If the Earth suddenly starts to speed up, we'd fall over backwards, and we'd have to lean into the direction of the motion to stand.

Chapter - 16

HOW FAR IS A STAR?

The innumerable stars that brighten a night sky are made up of hot gases. Even the Sun is a star. However, there are various other stars that are brighter than the Sun but cannot be seen by us. This is because of their distance from the Earth. Stars may look like tiny dots in the sky but are actually really big, some even bigger than planets. They appear small to us because they are very far away. Have you ever thought exactly how far stars are from the Earth?

The unit of measuring distance of stars is light years. One light year is referred to the distance travelled by light in one year, the velocity of light being three hundred thousand kilometers per second. The star nearest to the Earth is the Sun. It is followed by a star called the Proxima Centauri, whose distance from the Earth is about 4.28 light years. However, this star is only visible in the southern hemisphere.

The nearest star which is visible from the northern hemisphere is Sirius, also called the Dog Star. From the Earth, it is around 8.8 light years away. Apart from these, another important neighboring star is the Alpha Centauri, which is 4.37 light years away from our planet.

The star farthest from us which is visible to our naked eye is more than 8 million light years away from Earth. If a powerful telescope is used, one can see stars that are a 1,000 times more distant.

It may sound shocking but it is true that there are some stars in this universe that are so far away from us that their light takes more than a 1,000 million years to reach us.

Stars contain the greatest secrets about the universe. Studying the evolution of a star can help reveal many unknown facts about our galaxy and planet. It is due to this reason that since times immemorial, people have been curious about the tiny sparkles we enjoy gazing at in the night.

A Boy Looking at the Stars with a Telescope

From way back in time, people have been inventing newer devices to expose the secrets of stars. Over time, scientists have created a variety of *optical and radio telescopes* for the study of stars. They have been successful in gaining knowledge about these heavenly bodies, but there is still a lot which is yet to be discovered.

Quick Facts

- Stars are cosmic energy engines that produce heat, light, ultraviolet rays, x-rays, and other forms of radiations. They are composed largely of gases and plasma, a superheated state of matter composed of subatomic particles.
- Though the most familiar star, our Sun, stands alone, about three of every four stars exist as part of a binary system containing two mutually orbiting stars.
- No one knows how many stars exist, but the number would be staggering. Our universe likely contains more than 100 billion galaxies, and each of these galaxies may have more than 100 billion stars.
- Some stars have always stood out from the rest. Their brightness is a factor of how much energy they put out, which is called their luminosity, and also how far away from the Earth they are.
- Stars may occur in many sizes, which are classified in a range from dwarfs to supergiants. Supergiants may have radii a thousand times larger than that of the Sun.
- Hydrogen is the primary building block of stars. The gas circles through space in cosmic dust clouds called the Nebulae. In time, gravity causes these clouds to condense and collapse on themselves. As they get smaller, the clouds spin faster because of the conservation of angular momentum. Young stars are called Protostars. As they develop, they accumulate mass from the clouds around them and grow into what are known as main sequence stars. The main sequence stars like our Sun exist in a state of nuclear fusion during which they will emit energy for billions of years by converting hydrogen to helium.

Chapter - 17

THE MASS OF THE EARTH

Whenever a body has to be measured, it is done through the use of a **weighing balance**. The balance is in accordance with the object to be weighed. Our planet, Earth is a giant object. Hence, to weigh the Earth, thinking of a weighing scale is impossible.

An interesting story lies behind the weighing of the Earth.

Newton was a great scientist and made many advancements in the field of science. He introduced theories and laws that are widely used even today. Actually, scientifically, to weigh the Earth, *Newton's law of gravitation is used.*

This law states that there exists a force of attraction between any two bodies in the universe and this is dependent on the masses of the two bodies as well as on the distance between them. Moreover, the force of attraction is directly proportional to the product of the masses of the two bodies and inversely proportional to the square of distances between them.

Weighing the Earth

To determine the mass of the Earth, an experiment is conducted. It is done with the help of the above mentioned law.

Sir Isaac Newton

In the first step of this experiment, a small metallic ball is suspended with the help of a thin piece of thread. Then, the accurate position of the ball is determined. After this, a huge lead ball that weighs a ton is brought close to the ball. When this is done, the small ball is attracted towards the big lead ball and moves from its initial position. This change in position is due to the gravitational force. In this case, it is less than one-tenth of an inch.

This displacement can be accurately measured. It is done very accurately and carefully with the help of precision instruments.

Through this concept of measuring displacement, the mass of the Earth has been determined. The approximate mass of the Earth is calculated to be somewhere around 5980,000,000,000,000,000,000 tonnes!

Hence, it is only apt to say that to calculate the mass of the Earth is a very tough task and can be done only with the help of Science.

Quick Facts

- **The Earth is the biggest of all the terrestrial planets. A terrestrial planet is a dense planet found in the inner Solar System. The diameter of Earth is 7,926 miles. The circumference measured around the equator is 24,901 miles. There are currently almost 7 billion people living on the Earth. About 30% of the Earth's surface is covered with land, while about 70% is covered by oceans.**

- Our planet, the Earth is an oasis of life in an otherwise desolate universe. The Earth's temperature, weather, atmosphere and many other factors are just right to keep us alive.
- The Earth is about 4.5 billion years old.
- The size of the Earth is approximately 7,926.41 miles (12,756.32 km) in equatorial diameter.
- The surface area of the Earth is around 196,800,000 square miles (509,700,000 square km)
- The atmospheric composition of the Earth is: Nitrogen (78%), Oxygen (21%), Argon (0.9%), with other gases making up the remainder (0.1%).
- CRUST COMPOSITION: Oxygen (46.6%), silicon (27.7%), aluminum (8.1%), iron (5%), calcium (3.6%), sodium (2.8%), potassium (2.6%), magnesium (2%), and other elements making up the remainder.
- TEMPERATURE: Ranging from 136 degrees Fahrenheit (58 degrees Celsius) to –128.6 degrees Fahrenheit (-89.6 degrees Celsius). 57 degrees Fahrenheit (14 degrees Celsius) average
- ONE DAY: 23 hours, 56 minutes, 4.09 seconds (We round this to 24 hours.)
- ONE YEAR: 365 days, 6 hours, 9 minutes, 9.54 seconds (We round this upto 365 days)
- NATURAL SATELLITES: 1
- DISTINCTIVE FEATURE: Only planet that supports life.

Chapter - 18

THE TWINKLING OF STARS

One of the first things that a toddler learns is the famous rhyme, 'Twinkle twinkle little star...'

From the young ones to the elderly people, everybody enjoys gazing at the night sky at one time or the other. Their mesmerising sight has the power to appeal to the senses.

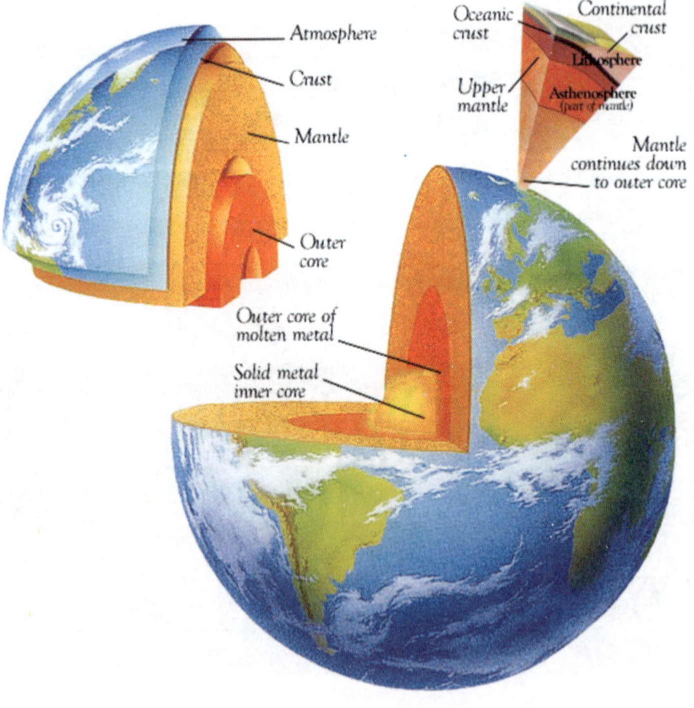

The Sun is also a Star

Stars radiate light in all directions. Though they appear small, some stars are even bigger than the Earth itself. Have you ever wondered why the stars in the sky twinkle?

The **atmosphere** blankets the Earth, protecting it from

harmful radiations that come from the outer space. Beyond it is a huge **vacuum**. The atmosphere consists of various gases which are always in motion. Due to their movements, the density of the atmosphere is never constant. Moreover, the refractive index of air varies from place to place.

The light of a star, after entering the Earth's atmosphere, gets deviated a number of times due to changing densities and consequent changes in the refractive index of the air.

Refraction refers to the degree of change or deviation in the path of light when it enters from one medium to the other. Indeed it is due to refraction that the stars twinkle. Due to changing refractive index of the air, the light coming from the stars gets refracted at different angles before reaching our eyes. This leads to the fluctuation of light entering into our eyes.

Knowing this, one may wonder why other planets or the moon does not twinkle. This is because while stars are smaller in size, planets are bigger. Stars can be considered as point-like structures in the night sky. However, planets are an extended source or a collection of the point size sources of light. So they cancel out the effect of twinkling.

The Twinkling Stars at Night

Also, due to larger angles, the deviation of the path of light from the moon and planets does not get detected by our eyes. Thus, they don't appear to twinkle.

Quick Facts

- The stars do not twinkle. Their light gets distorted by the churning gases in the Earth's atmosphere. We only notice the twinkling as stars are tiny points of light and are thousands of light-years away, whereas, planets don't twinkle as they're close enough to appear as tiny discs.
- Stars are generally huge balls of gases in outer space. Made from hydrogen, helium and other elements, stars produce light, heat and other forms of energy.
- Stars are in constant conflict with themselves. The collective gravity of all the mass of a star is pulling it inward. If there was nothing to stop it, the star would just continue collapsing for millions of years until it would become its smallest possible size; maybe as a neutron star.
- The nuclear fusion at the core of a star generates a tremendous amount of energy. The photons push outward as they make their journey from inside the star to reach the surface; a journey that can take 100,000 years. When stars become more luminous, they expand outward becoming red giants. And when they run out of the light pressure, they collapse down into white dwarfs.

Chapter - 19

THE FORCE OF GRAVITY

It is a known fact that there exists an invisible force on our Earth which pulls all objects towards the centre of the Earth. It is because of this force that everything that is thrown up comes back, and this force is called **gravity**.

Apple Falling due to Gravitational Force

The centre of gravity lies at the centre of the Earth. Hence, if a hole is drilled in the Earth, from one side to the other and an object is thrown inside from one side, it will stop at the centre due to gravity and not come out of the other end.

Also, the weight of a body will be more if it is close to the centre of the Earth. Similarly, the body would weigh less if it is away from it. This is the reason why *things weigh more at the Poles than at the Equator, because the Poles are closer to the centre of the Earth*.

Not only the Earth, but all the planets have this force of gravity. In fact, all objects of the universe attract each other. It is this force which keeps all the objects in their place. This force is also responsible for the revolution of the Moon around the Earth and the Earth around the Sun.

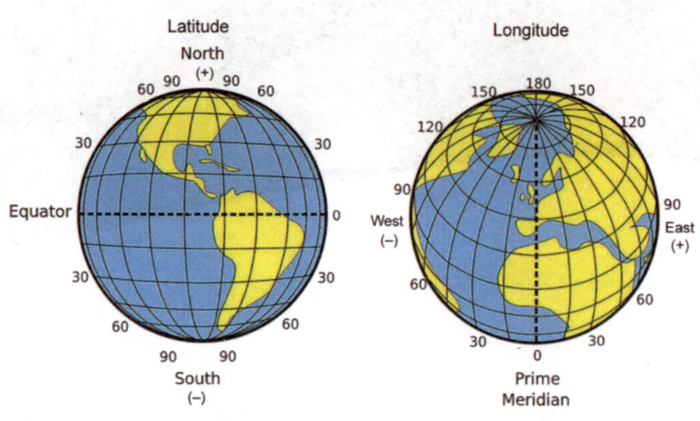

Globe showing Latitudes and Longitudes

It is obvious that the *Moon attracts the Earth*. This is the reason behind the *tides in the seas*.

Till the 16th century, it was believed that in vacuum, if two bodies were dropped from the same height simultaneously, the heavier body would hit the ground first. However, this assumption was broken by **Galileo Galilei**. He proved that irrespective of their masses, all objects dropped from the same point at the same time would hit the ground together in a vacuum.

He did so by throwing two balls of different masses from the Leaning Tower of Pisa in front of a thousand people.

Subsequently, Newton declared the law of gravity which states that, the force of attraction between two bodies is directly proportional to the product of their masses and inversely proportional to the square of the distance between them. Hence, if the mass of one of the two bodies is doubled, the force of attraction between them also doubles.

However, if the distance between two objects is doubled, the force of attraction between them will reduce by one-fourth of the initial value.

Quick Facts

- On Earth, the acceleration due to gravity is 9.8m/ sec^2
- The Universal Gravity Constant is 6.7e–11.
- Sir Isaac Newton came up with the idea of gravity when he saw an apple falling from a tree.
- The force of gravity decreases as you get farther away from the Earth.
- The force of gravity increases with the mass of the object.
- Gravity is caused as a result of space and time woven together.
- In a circular orbit, the centrifugal force is equal to the gravitational force.
- The force of gravity on the Moon is smaller than the force of gravity on the Earth.
- The gravitational force is smaller than the electric force when compared with the same mass.

Chapter - 20

ASTRONAUTS

Astronauts, also called *cosmonauts*, are highly trained professionals who travel to space. Explorers of the universe, these astronauts get trained by a human spaceflight program to become members of a spacecraft.

An Astronauts in Space

The first person to ever go into space was **Yuri Gagarin** in **1961**. He orbited around the Earth in 108 minutes. The first woman in space was **Valentina Tereshkova**, who orbited the Earth for almost 3 days. The youngest space traveller was **Gherman Titov**, who was 25 when he flew on a spacecraft. He was also the first to suffer 'space sickness.' On the other hand, the oldest astronaut was **John Glenn**, who flew at the age of 77.

Yuri Gagarin

For the execution of a project, different astronauts have different designations and duties.

- A Pilot Astronaut has the onboard responsibility of the crew, vehicle, success of the mission, and safety of the flight.

- A Mission Specialist Astronaut coordinates all the operations of the shuttle. They are expected to have a detailed knowledge of the shuttle and objectives of the mission as they perform extravehicular activities and assist in experiment operations.
- A Payload Specialist is an additional member to the crew who may be needed for certain specific tasks, depending upon the need of the operation.

While on a project, astronauts consume specially processed food which is easy to store and eat in the low-gravity environment. It is usually in the form of toothpaste tubes and contains all the vital nutrients that help to maintain the health of the astronauts.

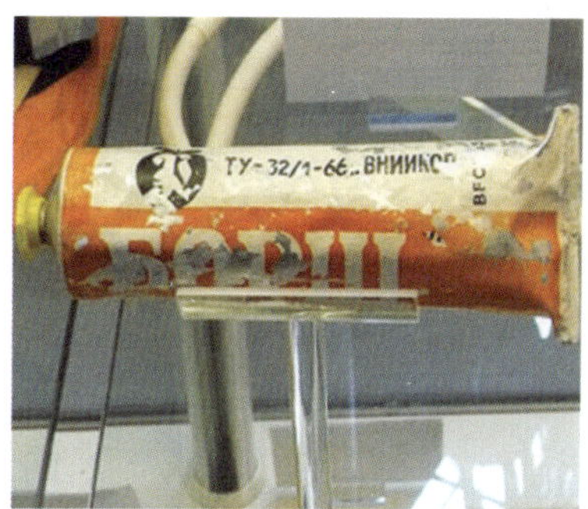

Food for Astronauts

The National Aeronautics and Space Administration (NASA) first selected astronauts for training in 1959. Although the requirements to become an astronaut today are very high, the first selected **John Glenn** and **Scott Carpenter**, of the **Mercury Seven Group**, did not have a college degree at the time of selection.

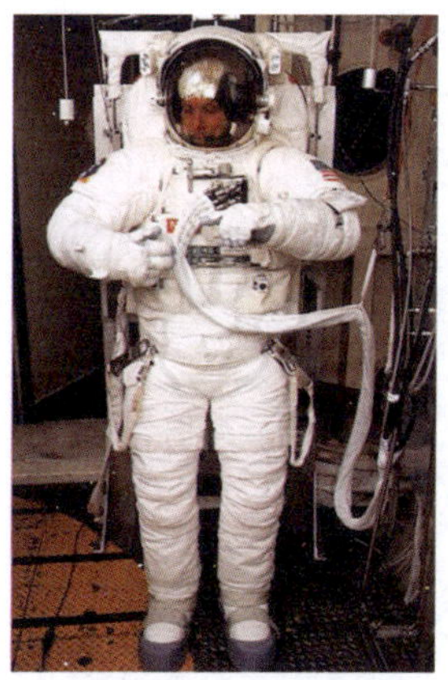

An Astronaut in Space Suit

In today's times, the NASA has laid down an extremely challenging requirement list for aspiring astronauts. The basic requirements for an astronaut include a bachelor's degree in engineering, biological science, physical science or mathematics, and at least 1,000 hours of pilot-in-command experience in a jet aircraft. Also, they are required to pass a physical test that includes distant visual acuity: 20/100, blood pressure: 140/90 measured in a sitting position and height between 62 and 75 inches.

After selection, the chosen astronauts go through an extensive training of 20 months to become competent of experiencing the conditions of space. This includes training for Extra-vehicular Activities (EVA) in the Neutral Buoyancy Laboratory, periods of weightlessness in the KC-135, also called the 'vomit comet', and flight experience of the T-38 jet aircraft.

Quick Facts

- **In space, it is not possible to breathe air normally, so an astronaut's spacesuit is outfitted with oxygen so that he/ she can breathe when working outside of the spacecraft.**
- **Astronauts can urinate while wearing their spacesuits outside the spacecraft. He or she usually wears a maximum absorbency garment (MAG), which can hold up to two litres of fluid.**
- **Astronauts sleep in bunk beds or in sleeping bags. However, these bunk beds must be fitted with buckles so that the astronauts can buckle up. Otherwise, they might float around the spacecraft while sleeping.**
- **Astronauts can choose from 70 different types of food. However, the food will either be already prepackaged for them or need just a very small amount of preparation. Sometimes, when the astronauts are eating, the food will float around, as there is no gravity.**
- **While not actively working, astronauts can read books, watch movies, or talk to family and friends on Earth. They can even use an exercise bike. (they have to do a lot of exercise to stay healthy.)**
- **The first living animal in orbit was a dog from Russia called Laika. It travelled into space on Sputnik 2 in 1957.**

PART - II

THE WORLD

Chapter - 1

THE STONE AGE

An Early Man

The Stone Age is that era in the history of mankind which is considered the landmark when human beings learnt to make use of **stone tools**. This age began more than three million years ago and lasted till around 5,000 years back. This age was followed by the **Bronze Age**. After this came the **Metal Age**, the time when man started using metals.

The Stone Age has broadly been classified into three periods:

- The Paleolithic or the Old Stone Age
- The Mesolithic or the Middle Stone Age
- The Neolithic or the New Stone Age

Old Stone Tools

The Old or the Paleolithic Stone Age is marked with the appearance of the first 'hominids' or man-like forms, for example, the Australopithecines. Men of this age were all hunters. They designed crude tools, made out of flaking stones. These tools date back to around 25,00,000 years ago. It is believed that apart from stones, woods and bones were also made use of to fabricate tools. The Pleistoce Epoch began 25,00,000 years back and lasted till 10,000 years back. It was during the latter part of this age that 'hominids' learnt the art of making paintings on caves and also the art of sculpture.

Early Man Making Clay Pots

The Mesolithic or the Middle Stone Age began around 8000 B.C., when certain advancement started in north-western Europe. This age saw betterment in the design of the stone tools. Hunters started using tiny *flint flakes* in making harpoons and *arrows*. This age ended in 2700 B.C.

The Neolithic or the New Stone Age saw further advancement as it marked the beginning of farming and the manufacture of pottery in Europe. This age began around 9,000 years ago in the Middle East. People of this time learnt to grind and polish stones and manufactured smooth axe heads. Moreover, agriculture and domestication of animals were among the most vital characteristics of the Neolithic Age.

It was also during this time that the practice of mining had begun. Agriculture had started and people had also begun forming villages. Soon after this period, people learnt making use of metals. This marked the end of the *Stone Age* and the beginning of the *Metal Age*.

When America was discovered by the Europeans, most of the Native Americans were living in the Neolithic Stone Age. In some parts of the world, people such as the Australian aborigines and the tribes in New Guinea continued to live in the Stone Age.

Quick Facts

- There are no written records from the Stone Age. What we know about the Stone Age humans comes from the things they made, like weapons, tools, shelters and other objects discovered mostly in archaeological digs. Engraving designs on stones and bones, carved figures and drawings on the walls of caves also give us information and help us trace the slow development of human beings or Homo sapiens throughout the period.
- The Stone Age is divided into Paleolithic, Mesolithic and Neolithic periods, marking the progressive levels of sophistication found in artifacts and cultural activities.
- The Paleolithic Age stretches from about 2-2.5 million years BCE to 10,000 years BCE, which is about 95 percent of the time humans and their direct ancestors have been residing on this planet.
- Food was obtained mostly by hunting, fishing and collecting wild plants, nuts and fruits.

Chapter - 2

THE INTERNATIONAL DATE LINE

It is a known fact that, with 15 degrees longitude for each hour, the Earth is divided into 24 one-hour zones. These 24 zones complete one full day on our planet. Moreover, since the Earth rotates eastward, the progression of time on the clock is westward around the world.

Thus, the occurrence of 12 o'clock noon in London happens five hours before it does in Washington D.C., which is 75 degrees west of London and eight hours earlier at San Francisco, which is 120 degrees west of London. Therefore, at the time it is noon in London, it is midnight at the International Date Line or the IDL.

A Globe Showing Latitudes and Longitudes

To define it in simple terms, the International Date Line can be referred to as an imaginary line, extending from the North Pole to the South Pole. On its way, it cuts through the Pacific Ocean. This line is extremely important as it is the entire time system that the world works on. Each day on the Earth begins and ends at the International Date Line. At whichever point it crosses over land or divides nations, it gets diverted to pass over the Pacific Ocean.

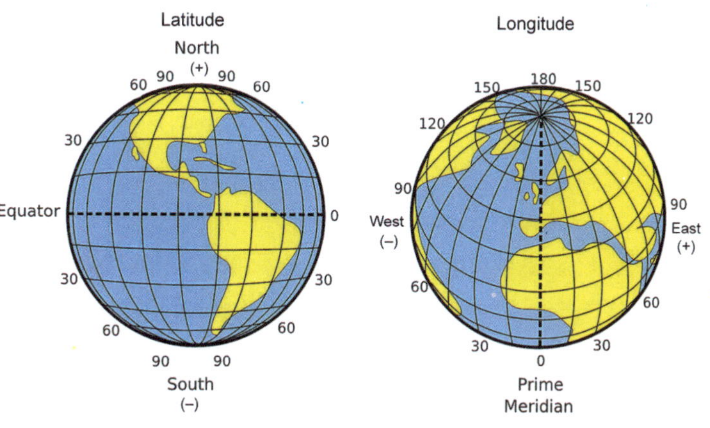

The Earth is divided into 360° Longitudes

This line is responsible for the deviation of east of the 180 degrees Longitude to pass through the Bering Strait and include the Eastern Siberia and then towards west to include the Aleutian Islands with Alaska. Towards the south of the Equator, the line again bulges eastward to let various island groups to experience the same day as New Zealand.

What needs to be understood is that the Earth is divided into 360 longitudes vertically, 180 on both eastern and western sides. The zero degree longitude passes through Greenwich and the *180 degrees longitude is called the International Date Line*. On either sides of this line, the time is the same, but with a difference of 24 hours. It is because of this that a person who is travelling in the westward direction across the line has to adjust his calendar back by one day.

In other words, it implies that if a person crosses the International Date Line while going eastward, he gains a day, while somebody travelling in the opposite direction loses a day.

Quick Facts

- The International Date Line (IDL) is an imaginary line that shows where the beginning of one day and the end of another come together. The Line is drawn vertically on maps and runs between the eastern tip of Russia and the western tip of Alaska, then down to the west of Hawaii, and then down to the east of New Zealand, and so on. It has several zigzags in it, too. It goes through no land except Antarctica.
- Points near the Line are almost 24 hours apart. When it is Tuesday in New Zealand, it is Monday in Hawaii. This is because the globe is divided into Time Zones that total to 24 hours. So, if you board a plane in Juneau, Alaska, on Monday and fly west to Tokyo, Japan, you will arrive on Tuesday. This is because the Earth is round.
- Many years went by before someone proposed a Date Line, opposite the Prime Meridian. It began to be drawn on maps as early as the 17th century and was not popularly adopted until much later.
- Even today, no law proclaims that an International Date Line exists. Still, most of the globes and maps of the world include it.

Chapter - 3

THE NAME, AMERICA

Today, the United States of America (USA) is the big brother of the world. Regarded as a superpower, America is one of the most powerful countries in the world. It has developed mainly in the past 100 years.

United States

Christopher Columbus

The story of the discovery of America is an interesting story. In the year 1492, the renowned Italian traveller, **Christopher Columbus** went on a sea voyage to search for India. On the morning of October 12, 1492, he arrived on an island which he named, 'San Salvador' after the King Ferdinand and Queen Isabella of Spain. Thinking it to be India, he called its inhabitants, **Indians**. This island is actually a part of America. It is presently known as the **Watling Island**.

Native Americans

Even though politically these people are **Native Americans** today, their descendants are often referred to as **Red Indians**. In his search for Japan, Christopher Columbus discovered **Cuba and Hispaniola**. On not being able to locate India, disappointed Columbus returned to Spain in the March of 1493.

Columbus set out on a second journey on September 24, 1493. This time he succeeded in discovering many **Virgin Islands**, such as **Jamaica** and **Puerto Rico**. However, his efforts to locate India once again went in vain.

During his third voyage in 1498, Columbus located **Trinidad** and touched upon **South America**. Around this time, a Florentine sailor called **Amerigo Vespucci** declared that he was the one to discover the mainland of South America on June 16, 1497.

In the year 1499, Amerigo Vespucci, along with Alonso de Ojeda sailed to Orinoco Straits and located **Venezuela**. Later, in the year, 1501-1502, Vespucci directed a voyage himself and discovered **Brazil** under the Portuguese banner.

Amerigo Vespucci

Soon, it became clear to Vespucci that what Christopher Columbus had discovered as India, was not a part of Asia but a different continent altogether. Vespucci started writing about this and these were widely spread during the beginning of 1500. He went on to become the first European to discover South America.

A German geographer named **Waldsee Miller**, to honour Amerigo Vespucci, named the territory of Brazil as South America. Today, the **North America** and **South America** are collectively referred to as the *Americas*.

Quick Facts

- **The United States of America (USA) is one of the largest countries in the world, based on both population and land area. It has a relatively short history compared to other world nations, has one of the world's largest economies, and has one of the world's most diverse populations. As such, the United States is highly influential internationally.**
- **The United States is divided into 50 states. However, each state varies in size considerably. The smallest state is the Rhode Island with an area of just 1,545 square miles (4,002 sq km). By contrast, the largest state by area is Alaska with 663,268 square miles (1,717,854 sq km).**
- **Alaska has the longest coastline in the United States at about 6,640 miles (10,686 km).**
- **The Bristlecone pine trees, believed to be some of the world's oldest living things, are found in the western United States in California, Utah, Nevada, Colorado, New Mexico and Arizona. The oldest of these trees is in California and the oldest living tree itself is found in Sweden.**

Chapter - 4

HOW WAS THE UK FORMED?

The United Kingdom comprises four main places which are **England, Wales, Scotland**, and **Northern Ireland**. It was formed in the year, 1801 when the 'Act of Union' enveloped Ireland under the same parliament as Scotland, Wales, and England.

The **Act of Union, 1801** described two complementary Acts, namely, the 'Union with Ireland Act 1800', an Act of the Parliament of Great Britain, and the 'Act of Union (Ireland) 1800', an Act of the Parliament of Ireland. It was passed on July 2, 1800 and August 1, 1800 respectively; the twin acts united

United Kingdom

the Kingdom of Great Britain and the Kingdom of Ireland to create the United Kingdom of Great Britain and Ireland. The union came into effect on January 1, 1801. Both acts together formed the United Kingdom, as we know it today.

In 1921, 26 Irish countries left the Union to form the *Irish Free State*, also known as the *Republic of Ireland*.

Five years later, in the year 1926, the 'Royal Parliamentary Titles Act' renamed the Union. It was then called the United Kingdom of Great Britain and Northern Ireland.

King Edward I

The system of government followed here is that of a constitutional monarchy and the monarchy is hereditary.

Wales, being subdued by **King Edward I** in 1282, was the first to unite with **England**. Ever since Edward gave his title to his son in 1301, the heir to the English throne is called The Prince of Wales. However, it was only in 1536, when **Henry VIII**, the Tudor monarch of Welsh descent passed an Act of Union that the principle was peacefully incorporated into the kingdom.

Great Britain was introduced as the name when King James VI of Scottish origin united and succeeded the English throne as **James I** in 1603 and the two crowns. However, he could not unite the nations.

Flag of United Kingdom

It was in the year, 1707 that another Act of Union brought Scotland and England under one government. The present flag of the United Kingdom consists of the flags of England (white with an upright red cross), the red vertical cross of Ireland, and the flag of Scotland (blue with a diagonal white cross).

The Royal Titles Act that was passed on May 29, 1953, issued the Queen the title of 'Elizabeth,, the second', by the Grace of God, of the United Kingdom of Great Britain and Northern Ireland and her other realms and territories, the Queen, the Head of the Commonwealth, the Defender of the Faith'.

Quick Facts

- **The United Kingdom or UK is a developed country and has the world's seventh-largest economy by nominal Gross Domestic Product (GDP) and the eighth-largest economy by purchasing power parity. It was the world's first industrialised country and the world's foremost power during the 19th and early 20th centuries.**
- **UK is presently recognised as a nuclear weapons' state and its military expenditure ranks fourth in the world.**
- **The United Kingdom has been a permanent member of the United Nations Security Council since its first session in 1946. It has been a member of the European Union and its predecessor, the European Economic Community since 1973. It is also a member of the Commonwealth of Nations, the Council of Europe, the G7, the G8, the G20, NATO, the Organisation for Economic Cooperation and Development (OECD) and the World Trade Organisation(WTO).**

Chapter - 5

THE CENSUS

The government takes a census every ten years to keep account of the population of a region. You may have noticed people coming to your house for a survey, asking about the number of family members, their age, gender, etc. This data is collected and organised. This process is called **census**.

Census of India

It is known that around *4000 B.C.*, the population of the world was around *85 million*. This proves that a census was taken at that time as well. The story behind the origin of census is unknown. However, another important aspect of the census is why it is taken. The reasons behind conducting census have changed with changing scenario of the world.

At the times of monarchy, the kings ordered for a census to assess the number of people available for wars. Another prime reason for conducting the census was for the collection of revenue. In earlier times, these were the two main reasons. However, over time, man has discovered many more uses of this process.

In today's times, one of the most important advantages of conducting a census is that it presents a clear picture of the demographics of the region it is conducted in. Aspects, such as health, education, income group, etc., can help the government in devising appropriate social schemes for the benefits of the society. A census also helps in judging the increase or decrease in the population of the region. Moreover, the birth rate can be determined and a ratio between rural and urban population can be calculated.

Due to these reasons, conducting a census becomes important for a country as it helps the government of a nation to act according to the need of the hour. The population count helps a nation determine if its provisions are adequate enough. Having an approximate idea of birth rate can help a nation prepare better for its future citizens. Lastly, the study of these demographics helps in elections as it is the population that decideds the number of voters in a particular constituency.

Apart from these direct implications, a census is very useful for the betterment of law and order and other socio-economic situations.

India conducted its first census in the year 1872. Since then, it is done

every ten years. The latest census of 2012 shows the population of India to be around 1.22 billion.

Quick Facts

- **The Census Act was passed in 1948 and was placed on the Statute Book. In 1949, the Government of India decided to initiate steps for the improvement of Registration of Vital Statistics and further decided to establish a single organisation at the Centre in the Ministry of Home Affairs under the Registrar General and ex-officio Census Commissioner for India to deal with Vital Statistics and Census.**
- **Till 1951, the Census Organisation in India was functioning like the phoenix, that is the Organisation came into being just on the eve of the census and established as soon as census operations were over within two or three years of its creation. With the establishment of a permanent nucleus at the centre, it has been possible to have continuing Census Organisation during the inter-censal period. Concentrated steps were taken to improve registration of births and deaths in the country to yield reliable vital rates which are so essential for the present day planning.**
- **The first census after Independence was taken in 1951. This report attempted to interpret the past changes in the size and structure of India's population and to point out their implications for the level of living of the population. The report also made a plea for reduction in the birth rate of the country. The 1951 census also attempted for the first time in the history of Indian census to make an assessment of the accuracy of the census count by a recheck in the field.**

Chapter - 6

THE FORMATION OF GRAND CANYON

Located in Arizona, U.S.A., the Grand Canyon is a **natural wonder of the world**. It is renowned for its spectacular view, the colourful rocks, and the majestic ambience. While travelling the Grand Canyon, one may imagine being lost in a city of rocks, with towers temples and castles in vibrant colours.

However, this panorama has a great history behind it. Have you ever wondered how The Grand Canyon was built? Well, here's the answer.

The Grand Canyon

The formation of the Grand Canyon is a result of continuous erosion of the Colorado River Valley. The immense force of the Colorado River cut out a great gorge thousands of years ago. Even now, each year the mighty force of the rushing water of this river continues to cut the bottom of this gorge deeper and deeper. This has made this the *deepest gorge in the world*.

Stretched up to 347.2 kilometers in length, the Grand Canyon is approximately 20 kilometers wide and up to 2 kilometers deep at certain places.

Since long ago, the Colorado River has been slowly cutting through the plateaus of northern Arizona, unleashing the strata of the Earth that is millions of years old. A subject of prime interest for geologists, is that these strata offer knowledge about the Earth's history.

An ancient *Precambrian rock* can be found at the bottom of the Canyon, where the Colorado River flows. It contains the fossils of primitive algae. In the higher strata, fossils of dinosaurs, elephants, trees, and other organisms can also be found. The top of the Canyon represents the most recent rocks. The fossils contained in the Canyon are extremely important as they provide useful insights into the evolutionary processes of the Earth's inhabitants.

The Grand Canyon is a top favourite for tourists. This spectacular site attracts more than two million tourists, each year. The Canyon offers its tourists a breathtaking view and a lot of mood swings that change just as the colour of the rocks.

In the year, 1919, the United States Government built the **Grand Canyon National Park** to promote and preserve the richness of plant and animal life that has become an integral part of this unique environment.

Quick Facts

- The geology of the Grand Canyon area exposes one of the most complete and studied sequences of rock on the Earth. The nearly 40 major sedimentary rock layers exposed in the Grand Canyon and in the Grand Canyon National Park area are about 200 million to nearly 2 billion years old. Most were deposited in warm, shallow seas and sea shores in western North America. Both marine and terrestrial sediments are represented, including fossilised sand dunes from an extinct desert. There are at least 14 known unconformities in the geological record found in the Grand Canyon area.
- Wetter climates brought upon by ice ages starting 2 million years ago greatly increased the excavation of the Grand Canyon, which was nearly as deep as it is now by 1.2 million years ago. Volcanic activity deposited lava over the area 1.8 million to 500,000 years ago. At least 13 lava dams blocked the Colorado River, forming lakes that were up to 2,000 feet (610 m) deep. The end of the last ice age and subsequent human activity has greatly reduced the ability of the Colorado River to excavate the canyon.
- However, in December 2012, a study published in the journal, *Science* claimed that new tests suggested that the Grand Canyon could be as old as *70 million years*.

Chapter - 7

THE STORY BEHIND MONA LISA

Mona Lisa Painting

The painting of **Mona Lisa** is one of the most renowned pieces of art the mankind has ever witnessed. Painted by Leonardo da Vinci, it is the portrait of a woman with a mysterious smile. The painting has left people wondering what she is smiling at. Today, the *Mona Lisa painting hangs in Paris at the Louvre Museum*, which preserves the world's finest art works and antiques.

This painting was made by **Leonardo da Vinci** between 1503 and 1506. The lady in the painting, Mona Lisa, was the wife of a Florentine gentleman, Francesco del Gioconda. She was 24 at the time, when the 51-year-old Leonardo started working on this painting. Mona Lisa used to come to his studio every day in the late afternoon, at the time the light was soft.

Leonoardo da Vinci

This painting was worked on for four years, during which Leonardo da Vinci became fascinated with both his model and the portrait. That is why this portrait has retained an exclusive ambience around itself.

Mona Lisa's face, charismatic and graceful, has amazed billions of people over the years. It seems like the painting has life in it. The background is mysteriously portrayed as a misty scenery.

King Francis

It is known that Leonardo da Vinci was so obsessed with the painting himself that he never gave it to Francesco. He always made an excuse and carried it with him wherever he went. It is also believed that while he was working on the painting, he used jesters, musicians, etc. to keep his model in a merry mood.

When Leonardo came to France in 1516, **King Francis** gave him a beautiful mansion in the Loire valley. He offered him 4,000 gold crowns for the painting but could not acquire it till Leonardo's death in 1519. Since then, the painting has been a possession of the emperors of France.

John F. Kennedy

It is remarkable that in the past 450 years, the painting has gone out of France only twice. In 1911, the painting was stolen, but found two years later in Italy. The second time, the painting went missing for 26 days, while it was taken during an amazingly well-guarded and immensely insured visit to the United States of America as a guest of the then **President, John F. Kennedy**.

Quick Facts

- Leonardo used a pyramid design to place the woman simply and calmly in the space of the painting. Her folded hands form the front corner of the pyramid. Her breast, neck and face glow in the same light that models her hands. The light gives various living surfaces an underlying spherical and circular geometry. Leonardo referred to a seemingly simple formula for the seated female figure: the images of seated Madonna, which were widespread at the time. He effectively modified this formula in order to create the visual impression of distance between the sitter and the observer. The armrest of the chair functions as a dividing element between Mona Lisa and the viewer.
- The woman sits markedly upright with her arms folded, which is also a sign of her reserved posture. Only her gaze is fixed on the observer and seems to welcome him to this silent communication. Since the brightly lit face is practically framed with various much darker elements (hair, veil, shadows), the observer's attraction to it is brought to even greater extent. The woman appears alive to an unusual measure, which Leonardo achieved by his new method by not drawing the outlines.
- Some art historians of the Eastern art, such as *Yukio Yashiro*, also argue that the landscape in the background of the picture was influenced by the *Chinese paintings*.

WHAT IS RED CROSS?

The Red Cross Flag

An international humanitarian organisation, called the **Red Cross Foundation** is devoted to alleviate all kinds of human suffering. The Red Cross has offices in almost all countries of the world that help people regardless of their sex, race, colour, etc. at times of both *peace and war*.

In times of peace, its goals are to provide first aid, provide safe drinking water, prevent accidents, train nurses, set up hospitals, establishing blood banks. On the other hand, at times of war, its main objective is to provide healthcare to wounded soldiers and victims.

Henri Dunant

The origin of this organisation is very engaging. The founder of Red Cross, **Henri Dunant**, a *Swiss banker* had gone to the city of **Lombardy in Italy** for business in 1859. The city at that time was the focus of the 'Battle of Solferino', between Australia and France.

Dunant witnessed thousands of wounded people, desperate for help, lying all around the roads. He was overwhelmed by the sight and regardless of his work, he started setting up local healthcare centres in association with the villagers. He saved many lives through his actions.

Three years after the war, Dunant wrote a book called, 'A Memory of Solferino', appealing to the people of the world to form relief societies for people affected by war. His idea gained worldwide recognition and in the International Conference of 1864 held in **Geneva**, **16 countries** agreed to set up the **Red Cross Societies**.

Thus, the Red Cross came into existence. It came to be known as the organisation whose motive is to relieve people from their sufferings caused by any kind of calamity.

The Red Cross has three organs. First is the *International Committee* which consists of *25 citizens of Switzerland*. Its main office is in Geneva. The second is the *League of the Red Cross Foundation* and the third is the *National Red Cross Society*.

At times of war, the International Committee looks after the prisoners of war and arranges for their proper healthcare. It also helps them connect to their relatives.

It also serves the people affected by natural disasters, such as, cyclones, tsunamis, etc. The Red Cross Organisation, in another word, is a *friend to humanity*.

Quick Facts

- The International Red Cross and Red Crescent Movement, born of a desire to bring assistance without discrimination to the wounded on the battlefield endeavours, in its international and national capacity, to prevent and alleviate human suffering wherever it may be found. Its purpose is to protect life and health and to ensure respect for the human beings. It promotes mutual understanding, friendship, cooperation and lasting peace among all the people.
- It makes no discrimination as to nationality, race, religious beliefs, class or political opinions. It endeavours to relieve the suffering of individuals, being guided solely by their needs, and to give priority to the most urgent cases of distress.
- It is a voluntary relief movement not prompted in any manner by desire for gain.
- There can be only one the Red Cross or one Red Crescent Society in any one country. It must be open to all. It must carry on its humanitarian work throughout its territory.
- The International Red Cross and the Red Crescent Movement, in which all Societies have equal status and share equal responsibilities and duties in helping each other, is worldwide.

THE SEVEN WONDERS OF THE ANCIENT WORLD

The world's most exquisite and wonderful architectural creations are referred to as the *Wonders of the World*. These wonders can be broadly classified into two categories – *the seven wonders of the ancient world* and the seven wonders *of the modern world*.

The wonders of the ancient world were regarded as magnificent creations of early civilisations by the Romans and the Greeks. The ancient seven wonders of the world consist of the following:

- *The Pyramids of Egypt*
- *The Hanging Gardens of Babylon*
- *The Tomb of Mausolus*
- *The Temple of Artemis (Diana)*
- *The Colossus of Rhodes of Helios*
- *The Statue of Zeus*
- *The Light House of Pharos near Alexandria*

The Pyramids of Egypt: The Great Pyramid of Giza (also known as the Pyramid of Khufu or the Pyramid of Cheops) is the oldest and

largest of the three pyramids in the **Giza Necropolis** bordering what is now **El Giza, Egypt**. It is the oldest of the Seven Wonders of the Ancient World, and the only one to remain largely intact. Egyptologists believe that the pyramid was built as a tomb for the fourth dynasty Egyptian Pharaoh Khufu (Cheops in Greek) over a 10 to 20-year period concluding around 2560 BCE. Initially at, 146.5 metres (481 feet), the Great Pyramid was the tallest man-made structure in the world for over 3,800 years. Originally, the **Great Pyramid** was covered by casing stones that formed a smooth outer surface; what is seen today is the underlying core structure. Some of the casing stones that once covered the structure can still be seen around the base. There have been varying scientific and alternative theories about the construction techniques of Great Pyramid. Most accepted construction hypotheses are based on the idea that it was built by moving huge stones from a quarry and dragging and lifting them into place.

Great Pyramid of Giza

There are **three known chambers** inside the Great Pyramid. The lowest chamber is cut into the bedrock upon which the pyramid was built and was unfinished. The so-called Queen's Chamber and the King's Chamber are higher up within the pyramid structure. The **The Great Pyramid of Giza** is the only pyramid in Egypt known to contain both ascending and descending passages. The main part of the Giza complex is a setting of buildings that included two mortuary temples in the honour of Khufu (one close to the pyramid and the other near the Nile), three smaller pyramids for Khufu's wives, an even smaller 'satellite' pyramid, a raised causeway connecting the two temples, and small mastaba tombs surrounding the pyramid for the nobles.

The Hanging Gardens of Babylon: These were one of the Seven Wonders of the Ancient World, and the only one of the wonders that may have been purely legendary. They were purposely built in the ancient city-state of Babylon, near present-day Al Hillah, Babil province, in Iraq. The Hanging Gardens were not the only World Wonder in Babylon; the city walls and obelisk attributed to Queen Semiramis were also featured in the ancient list of Wonders. The gardens were attributed to the Neo-Babylonian king Nebuchadnezzar II, who ruled between 605 and 562 BC. He is reported to have constructed the gardens to please his homesick wife Amytis of Media, who longed for the plants of her homeland. The gardens were said to have been destroyed by several earthquakes after the 2nd century BC. The Hanging Gardens of Babylon are documented by ancient Greek and Roman writers, including Strabo, Diodorus Siculus, and Quintus Curtius Rufus. However, no cuneiform texts describing the Hanging Gardens are extant, and no definitive archaeological evidence concerning their whereabouts have been found.

Hanging Gardens of Babylon

Tomb of Mausolus

The Tomb of Mausolus: One of the Seven Wonders of the Ancient World, the mausoleum was the tomb of Mausolus, from where the name came, and it was the most enduring achievement of his wife and sister Artemisia, the Younger, who, after Mausolu's death in 352 BC, had it built in his honour. Mausolu's tomb became one of the most famous architectural showpieces of antiquity; it was named one of the *Seven Wonders of the World by the travel writers* of the *Hellenistic era*. It consisted of a solid rectangular base topped by 36 Ionic columns. These were surmounted by a pyramid and crowned with a massive statue of Mausolus and Artemisia riding a chariot, reaching a total height of 60 metres. The base was adorned with a frieze executed by four of the leading sculptors of ancient Greece, one per side; classical writers were most impressed by these sculptures.

For at least the last 20 years, a Danish team of archaeologists and conservators, led by Prof. Kristian Jeppesen of the Aarhus University in Denmark, has been excavating and preserving the little remains of the site, consisting on the funerary underground chamber and architectural remains, many of them were found in the vicinity and the castle. The Mausoleum Museum was opened in 1988, thanks to the joint auspices of the Turkish and Danish governments, now under the management of the *Bodrum Museum of Underwater Archaeology*.

The Temple of Artemis: Also known less precisely as the *Temple of Diana*, was a Greek temple dedicated to a **goddess,** Greeks identified as **Artemis** and was one of the Seven Wonders of the Ancient World. It was located in Ephesus (near the modern town of Selçuk in present-day Turkey), and was completely rebuilt three times before its eventual destruction in 401. Only foundations and sculptural fragments of the latest of the temples at the site remain.

Temple of Artemis

The Colossus of Rhodes: This was a statue of the *Greek Titan Helios*, erected in the city of Rhodes on the *Greek island of Rhodes* by *Chares of Lindos* between 292 and 280 BC. It is considered one of the Seven Wonders of the Ancient World. It was constructed to celebrate Rhodes' victory over the ruler of Cyprus, Antigonus I Monophthalmus, whose son unsuccessfully besieged Rhodes in 305 BC. Before its destruction in the earthquake of 226 BC, the Colossus of Rhodes stood over 30 metres (107 ft) high, making it one of the tallest statues of the ancient world.

Colossus of Rhodes

Statue of Zeus

The Statue of Zeus: This statue was located on the west coast of *Greece at Olympia*. In the antiquity, this city was a place of cult which contained numerous treasures of the Greek art: temples, monuments, altars, theaters, statues and marble or bronze votive offerings. It was realised with golden and ivory, measured 12 m (39 feet) height and was placed on a base of 2 m (7 feet). The base of the statue was 6 m (21 feet) wide and 1 m height. The statue's perimeter was 13 m (43 feet). This work touched almost the ceiling of the temple. On the other hand, the throne was decorated with precious stones, ivory, ebony and gold.

Zeus, in the sitting position, holds, in its right hand, the goddess of Victory, Nike, and, in the left hand, a scepter surmounted by an eagle. The throne was decorated with relief sculptured mythological scenes, notably evoking the murder of the sons of Niobe, the Queen of Thebes.

The Light House of Pharos near Alexandria: The Lighthouse was built on the Island of Pharos in the harbour of Alexandria, Egypt. It was built around 290 BCE. It was a working lighthouse that helped ships find their way safely into the harbour. It was also a tourist attraction. Visitors could buy food at the observation platform on the first level. Anyone who wished to could climb nearly to the top. There were not many places in the ancient world that visitors could climb a man-made structure, 300 feet up, to view the sea.

Light House of Pharos

The Lighthouse stood for over 1500 years. Scientists believe an earthquake topped the Lighthouse during the 1300's. Divers today search for remains at the bottom of the Mediterranean Sea. It was situated in Egypt, near Alexandria. Made out of white marble, it was constructed in 279 B.C. and was 122 metres high. It remained till 796 A.D. of these, only *The Pyramids of Egypt are intact today*.

Quick Facts

- The construction of these wonders is an interesting story. The surviving Pyramids of Egypt were built around 5,000 years back. They were the tombs of the ancient Pharos or Kings.
- The biggest Pyramid is located near Cairo, in a town called Giza. This was the tomb of Pharaoh Cheops and his queen. Spread across an area of 5 hectares, its base forms a square and is approximately 147 meters high. The construction of this tomb of Pharaoh Cheops took over one lakh labourers and about 20 years.
- The Hanging Gardens of Babylon were built in the 9th century B.C. by King Nebuchadnezzar for his wife Amytis. Built with a series of terraces, one on top of the other, they were 7.6 metres thick and trees grew on each terrace. Irrigation in these high gardens was done through pumping water from river Euphrates. After the Persians took control of the place, people left as it was in ruins.
- The third wonder, The Tomb of Mausolus was built by the ruler of Halicarnassus, King Marsolus. Though he died before the tomb was completed, his wife Artemesia looked into its construction. It was 42.6 meters high with a statue of the king and queen riding a horse chariot. It eventually collapsed but its remains are preserved in the British Museum, London.
- The Temple of Artemis (Diana) of Ephesus with its roof rested on two rows of approximately 200 metres high, was constructed in the honour of the Goddess in 550 B.C. A mad man burnt it down in 365 B.C. Alexander the Great rebuilt it in 250 B.C.

Exercises

I. Answer the following questions.

Q.1. What does the atmosphere consist of?

Q.2. What are the different layers of the atmosphere? Name and explain them briefly.

Q.3. "An apple a day, keeps the doctor away." Does an apple actually have the properties to keep all diseases at bay? What does this proverb actually mean?

Q.4. List about five uses of apple.

Q.5. What is Paresthesia, which is also referred to as 'Pins and Needles'?

Q.6. What are general symptoms of Paresthesia, and how can we overcome the disease?

Q.7. What causes the change of seasons and how many seasons do we usually have?

Q.8. Who proposed the theory of the 'Survival of the Fittest'? What was explained in his theory?

Q.9. Why have some of the plants and animals become extinct?

Q.10. Why are owls known as 'Nocturnal Creatures'? What are the factors that enable them to see clearer during the night time?

Q.11. What do you understand by the term, 'Migration'? Why do the birds have to migrate?

Q.12. Can you name two Migratory Birds and the places to which they migrate?

Q.13. What are Fireworks and where were they first manufactured? Explain their chemical composition.

Q.14. How are Rainbows formed and what are the different colours in a rainbow?

Q.15. What all does Milk contain? Why should children drink milk every day?

II. Fill in the blanks with suitable words.

1. An optical instrument called a ________ is a tube-like tool used to see distant objects with magnified clarity.
2. The telescope was invented in 1608 by________, a ________ optician.
3. Telescopes are mainly of three types: ______________, ______________ and ____________.
4. The temperature of a star determines its _______and __________. If the temperature of the star is high, its brightness ___________.
5. __________was the first scientist to successfully measure distances beyond our galaxy, the Milky Way or 'Akash Ganga' as it is called in Indian Astronomy.
6. The ________is known as a guiding star as it leads man to his bearings.
7. One of the many wonderful things about stars is that one can determine _______ with their help.
8. The _________calendar is today's internationally accepted civil calendar and is also known as the 'Western calendar' or the 'Christian calendar'.
9. A Polish astronomer, named _____________ put forth his theory of the Earth's revolution around the Sun.
10. It was hence proved that the ________ revolves around the Sun and completes one full revolution in________________.

III. Match the two columns correctly.

	A	B
1.	One rotation gets completed in 24 hours.	by the Earth's rotation.
2.	The Earth rotates and revolves at the same time, but we don't feel any motion	and this makes one full day.
3.	The day and night are caused	is the Sun.
4.	The change of seasons occurs	due to its revolution.
5.	The unit of measuring distance of stars	is light years.
6.	The star nearest to the Earth	is Sirius, also called the Dog Star.
7.	The nearest star visible from the northern hemisphere	because of the force of gravity.
8.	Whenever a body has to be measured,	that the stars twinkle.
9.	It is due to refraction only	we use a weighing balance.
10.	Tides occur in the seas	because the Moon also attracts the Earth.

IV. Multiple Choice Questions (MCQs)

1. Sir Isaac Newton declared:

   a. the law of gravity b. the Boyle's law c. the Charles law

2. The first person to ever go into space in 1961 was:

   a. Neil Armstrong b. Yuri Gagarin c. John Glenn

3. The first woman in space was____________, who orbited the Earth for almost three days.

   a. Valentina Tereshkova b. Sunita Williams

   c. Kalpana Chawla

4. The Stone Age is considered to be the landmark when human beings learnt to make use of:

   a. Metals b. Stone weapons c. Stone tools

5. Each day on the Earth begins and ends at the:

   a. International Date Line b. Prime Meridian

   c. Equator

6. America is one of the most powerful countries in the world. It has primarily developed in the past:

   a. 50 years b. 70 years c. 100 years

7. America was discovered by a renowned Italian traveller named:

   a. Christopher Columbus b. Vasco da Gama

   c. Magellan

8. The United Kingdom consists of four main places which are England, Wales, Scotland and Northern Ireland and was formed in the year:

   a. 1701 b. 1601 c. 1801

9. The UK has been a permanent member of the ________ since its first session.

   a. United Nations Security Council

   b. European Union

   c. NATO

10. India conducted its first census in the year________ and since then, it is done every 10 years.

    a. 1879 b. 1872 c. 1874

Glossary

Aberration: A deviation from the proper or expected course; abnormal

Contentious: Something that can be argued

Diurnal Birds: Birds which see better in the day than at night

Fermentation: The process of conversion of sugars into ethanol; fermentation of milk leads to the preparation of curd.

Galactic: Within a galaxy

Homogenised: The process of reducing fat from milk

Nocturnal Birds: Birds which see better during the night than in daytime

Poaching: Illegal hunting

Predicament: A problem

Renowned: Well known

Rods and cones: Special cells which help in the clarity of vision

Pyramid: A massive monument of ancient Egypt with rectangular base and four triangular faces

Lighthouse: A tall structure tapped by a powerful light as signal to help boats and ships

Harbour: A sheltered port for anchoring a ship

Obsessed: Preoccupied; inclined excessively

Immensely: Extremely large; tremendously